wings n' things
a handbook
of creative
crafts activities
janice a piscitelli
Parker Publishing Company, Inc.
West Nyack, New York

Dedication

I feel great joy in dedicating this book to my mother, Lia, and my father, Clem. Their love, encouragement and guidance has influenced my life in immeasurable proportions.

Acknowledgements

A very special thank you to the many children who have inspired me to write this book. With their invaluable repertoire of ideas and relentless creative energy, my motivational fuel was in boundless supply. Additionally, I want to thank my wonderful family and special friends and teachers who have made the manifestation of this book a joyous reality.

thank you ♥ thank you ♥ thank you ♥

PARKER PUBLISHING COMPANY, INC.

West Nyack, N.Y.

Library of Congress Cataloging in Publication Data

Piscitelli, Janice A.,
Wings n' things.

1. Creative activities and seat work—Handbooks, manuals, etc. 2. Handicrafts—Handbooks, manuals, etc. I. Title.
LB1537.P57 1983 372.5 83-11432

ISBN 0-13-960559-2

Printed in the United States of America

about the author

FOREWORD

This craft guide has been written to assist both teacher and student in developing visually successful art products while encouraging creative growth through divergent thinking. It is the intention of these lessons to elevate the area of crafts to a level which denies rote processes, yet implants developmental acquisition of skills in combination with individualized ideas. Geared toward the elementary and junior high school curriculae, crafts have been purposefully selected as an alternative, rather than as a replacement, for teaching areas considered as fine arts. The implementation of the lessons selected will provide the children with invaluable tools, equipping them with the foundations needed in many areas of the arts. The encouragement of alternative methods of problem solving will extend itself far beyond the art room walls and into the fabric of everyday learning.

As a means of nurturing a positive attitude within the child, the lessons foster a personally satisfying product using an investigative process. When the child experiences success, feelings of self-confidence are generated. With repetitions of successful learning experiences, the child will be encouraged to implement a very personal creative response. The teacher should promote inquisitive investigation by approaching each project with a mind open to alternative possibilities offered by the child. While basic techniques should be defined clearly, with emphasis on quality craftsmanship and design principle, variation and extension of methods should also be employed.

This guide has been divided into areas dealing with the folding process, ceramics, papier-mâché, mobiles, soft art, and puppetry. Each section should be read from the beginning, as a continuity is made available in both concept and application of knowledge investigated in earlier lessons. Experimentation is recommended, so that materials, size and embellishment be treated with variety to achieve creative results. Ideas may be used in combination with each other or as a supplement to previously acquired skills. A combination of functional art and visual wonders are included, so that the children may develop a sense of art appreciation as well as an achievement of a serviceable item.

about the creative response

Art is a collection of experiences. It assimilates emotional, perceptual and intellectual life experiences. The child sorts out, eliminates, integrates, associates and recreates in making things. The way something works or what it represents in the mind of the child is as critical as what it looks like after he or she creates it in concrete form. Creativity is a natural, inherent response to problem solving or expression in its own realm. Creative response is not confined to the studio nor isolated visual response. It is a living, vital reaction to an odyssey of ongoing living, learning experiences. It is as individual as the fingerprint and manifests itself in a developmental manner with the growth of each child.

Art in the classroom need not be restricted by limited funds. A hodgepodge of seemingly unrelated collectables may be translated into high caliber pieces. Art can be made from recycled materials and materials can be recycled in art. The creative eye will find workable media in any environment, be it from the supermarket, the lumberyard or the local attic. In combination with basic tools and supplies, the list of creations are only bounded by the walls of the imagination.

WORKING WITH KIDS

The best part about teaching art to kids is that it is self generating. One idea propels another into boundless action. Once the motivational thrust is launched in combination with just-right guidance, sufficient challenge, perfect organization and exact coaching, an avalanche of ideas will inevitably follow. Kids love to concoct ideas built on previous experience. Allowed freedom to activate their ideas within the bounds of taught skills and craftsmanship, children will astound you with excitingly unpredictable responses. Unhampered by many pre-conceived mental roadblocks acquired with years, the child goes full steam ahead in implementing her evocative masterpieces. Provided with tools of learning and helpful guidance, the child will approach the concept presented with ideas lent by subject matter and media. Clay, for example, will make good wind chimes because of what it will do and how it will do it. Knowing about the qualities of a material will assist the child in applying his own ideas within the working realms of that media. The most exciting part is when the child comes up with her own selection of media based on the nature of the creative endeavors. The art teacher has the profound joy of re-activating that electrical impulse lying just beneath the surface of much conventional subject matter. With the child, the teacher shares the joys of dynamic spontaneity created from a junk heap of odds n' ends. Together, the teacher and child grow and respond to one another, kindling the fire that ignites the world of infinite creations!

Aaaah —— artistic combustion!

caution caution caution

Care must be excercised in using potentially dangerous tools such as X-ACTO and utility knives and metal cutters, which are called for in a few of the activities in this book.

Be sure to give careful instructions before handing out these tools, and to warn your students about the hazards of misuse.

contents

★ represents a new unit

★ SAVE ★ SAVE ★ SAVE ★ SAVE ★ SAVE ★

♥ Start gathering free art supplies!

- cereal boxes
- corrugated cardboard boxes
- shoe boxes
- oatmeal and salt boxes
- paper towel tubes
- toilet paper tubes
- egg cartons
- milk containers
- plastic containers
- aluminum trays
- styrofoam trays
- shirt cardboards
- styrofoam packing
- detergent bottles
- wide mouth jars
- wallpaper samples
- paper bags
- twine and string
- spools
- bottle caps
- wire coat hangers
- tin cans
- nylon stockings
- old socks
- old stuffed toys
- old pillows
- old upholstery fabric
- sample fabric books
- wood scraps
- bones
- shells
- driftwood
- pinecones
- old jewelry
- old hats
- nut shells
- outgrown clothes
- remnant fabric
- magazines
- feathers
- sticks
- old lace
- nuts, bolts, nails, screws
- seeds
- dried weeds, flowers
- newspaper
- screening
- old tablecloths

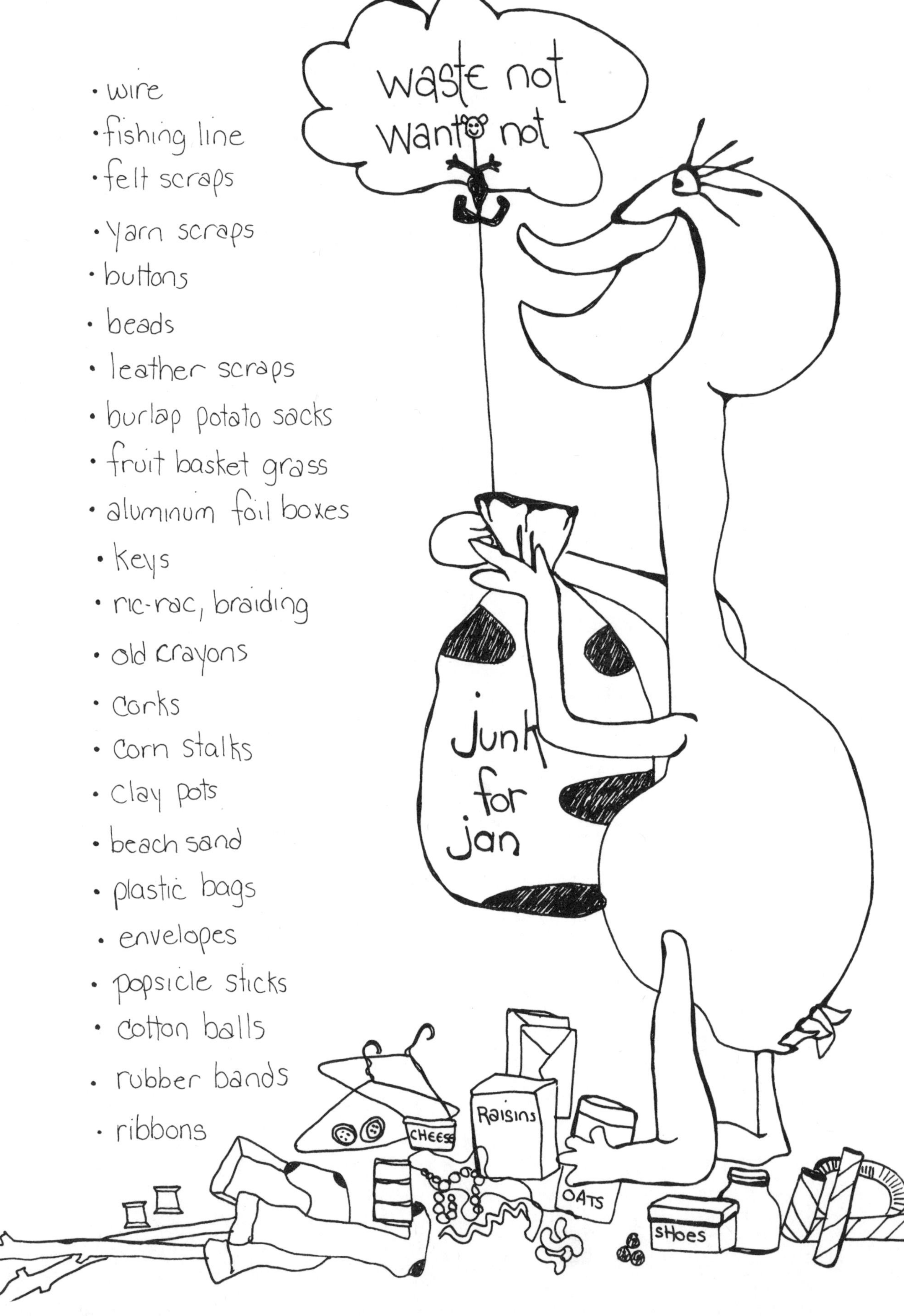
• wire
• fishing line
• felt scraps
• yarn scraps
• buttons
• beads
• leather scraps
• burlap potato sacks
• fruit basket grass
• aluminum foil boxes
• keys
• ric-rac, braiding
• old crayons
• corks
• corn stalks
• clay pots
• beach sand
• plastic bags
• envelopes
• popsicle sticks
• cotton balls
• rubber bands
• ribbons
waste not
want not
Junk
for
jan
CHEESE
Raisins
OATS
SHoes

cutting on the fold

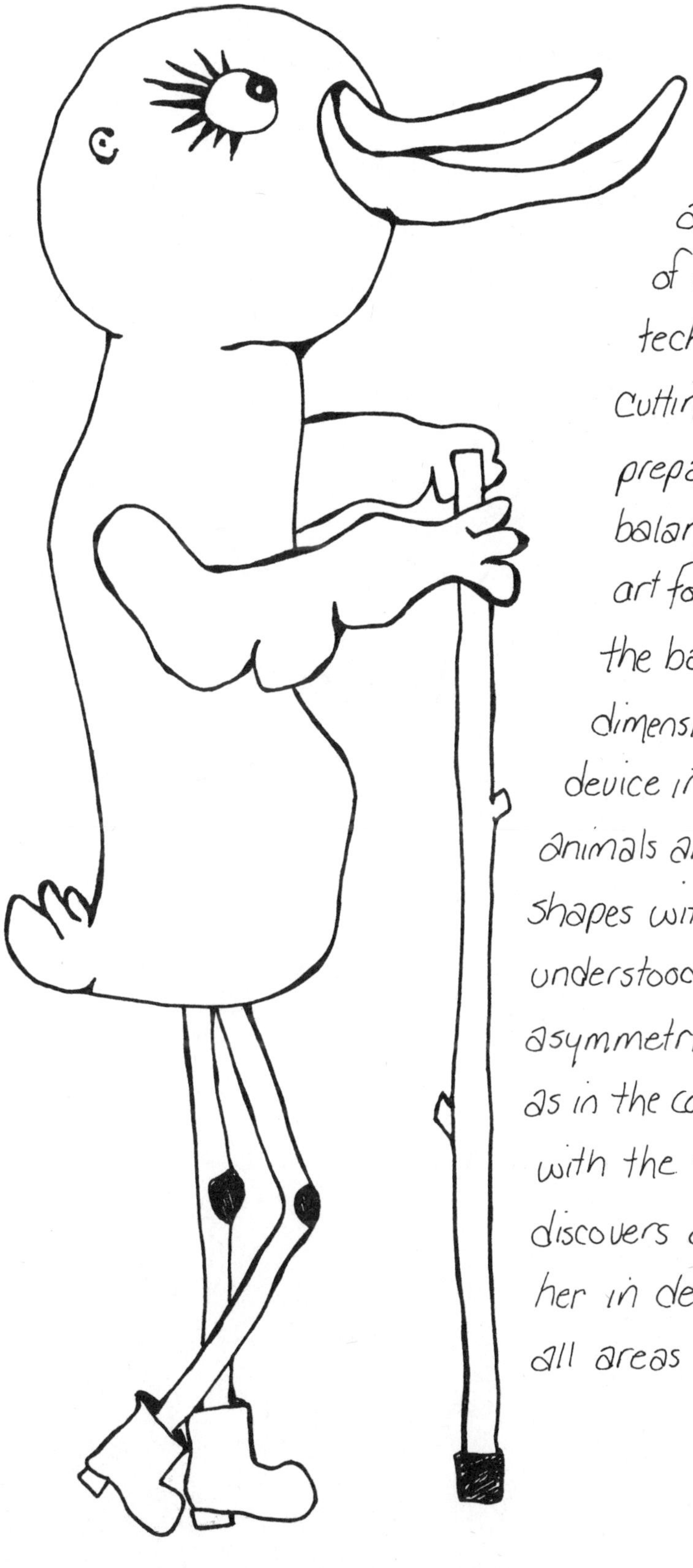

A special section has been written on the use of the folding process in art activities, as it lends itself to an assortment of different projects. As an expedient technique for attaining symmetry, cutting shapes off the fold of a paper prepares the child for the use of balance as a central component in art form. Symmetrical shapes may be the basis for both two- and three-dimensional studies. Folding is an invaluable device in the construction of masks, stand-up animals and in appreciating the delicacies of shapes within a snowflake. As balance is understood through symmetrical forms, asymmetrical balance may be introduced, as in the construction of mobiles. In working with the folding process, the young artist discovers a technique which will assist her in developing creative aesthetics in all areas of construction.

hex signs

Hex signs are traditionally associated with the Pennsylvania Dutch. They were used to ward off evil or bring good fortune. Hex signs can be created on any circular background – you can use enamels on Masonite or tissue on paper plates.

Paper plate hexes: 1. Fold colored tissue paper 3 times; draw a shape on fold and cut it out - you'll have 4 shapes.

2. Make more identical shapes, arranging all shapes symmetrically.

3. Glue with rubber cement.

4. Using fine tipped markers, add details. Hang with yarn.

pinwheels

1.

You can decorate one side with oil pastels-it's a nice effect.

9"

9"

I don't know of anyone who isn't fascinated by pinwheels. They're such a joy on a breezy day and so simple to make!

2.

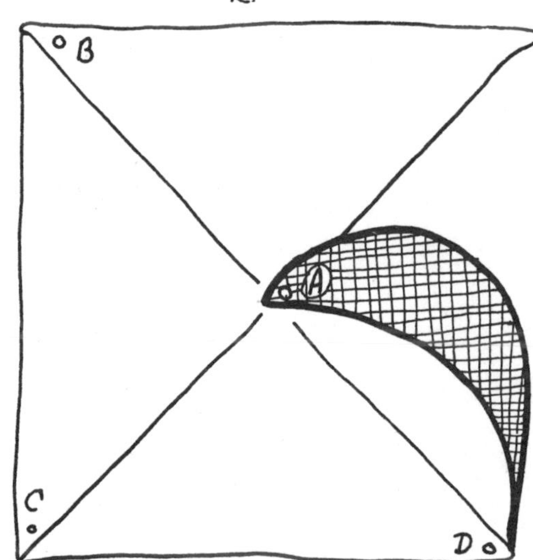

Blow into them if there's no breeze.

Vinyl Wallpaper Samples work really well ... they're dazzling!

huge ones make great displays!

1. Divide a 9" square of construction paper as shown and cut almost to center. (o)
2. Bring points A, B, C and D to center and secure to a stick with a small nail pushed through a thin cardboard circle.

PEOPLE IN OUR WORLD

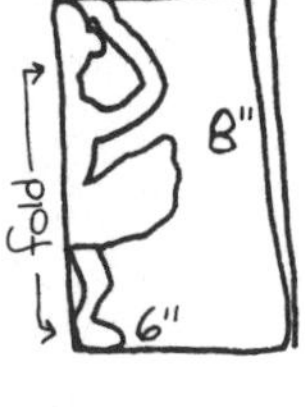

8"

fold

6"

Donald Elly Amy Sam Janet Linda Tommy Susan Patti Kay Frank Cathy Corine Mark Becky Julie Elise

It's a SMALL SMALL WORLD !!!

This is a fun way to introduce children to one another! Each child makes a paperdoll of herself, and you glue them around a large circle. Have the kids make themselves wearing their favorite costumes. Use oil pastels on construction paper and authenticate costumes with scraps.

torn art

experiment with lots of different types of line.

fold

An ALTERNATIVE TO SCISSORS to STRETCH YOUR imagination!

Beautiful torn shapes not only free you from that required precision of scissors, but also enable you to delve into your limitless imaginative resources —— just like watching herds of elephants stampede across the sky on a breezy summer afternoon. Simply fold a piece of paper in half, tear a shape on the fold, then read into it. Rubber cement it to a background and turn it to life with felt-tipped markers and scraps.

sunsets

African images are used in this one.

2

fold

fold

fold

Strong Silhouette Shapes are really effective against a pastel tissue background. Choose a simple theme and explore the art of scissor cutting - the Chinese were Masters!

1. Make a frame by folding a sheet of black construction paper in half... cut a smaller rectangle out and glue a sheet of madras or rainbow tissue paper to fit inside.
2. Make fold and cut forms by folding rectangles of black construction paper and making half the shape on the fold. Sections may be removed from the main shape with an X-ACTO knife.
3. Arrange shapes on tissue background and glue down. Shapes may be overlapped.

handle X-ACTO with care!

please!!

Stained glass

A feeling of stained glass is achieved with construction paper filled with brightly colored cellophane or tissue.

fold

tissue or cellophane

Make small ones and tape to windows as ornaments. Larger, more intricate designs can be created from long panels of paper, using an X-ACTO knife for greater detail.

fold

light shining through illuminates colors!

★ Caution→ use care in handling X-ACTO knives-they're sharp! ★

1. Fold a rectangle of black construction paper in half. Draw a symmetrical form (half of it) on fold. Draw shapes within fold, starting and ending on fold. Cut out.
2. Glue colored tissue paper or cellophane onto back side of open areas. Glitter may be applied to front.

holiday wreaths

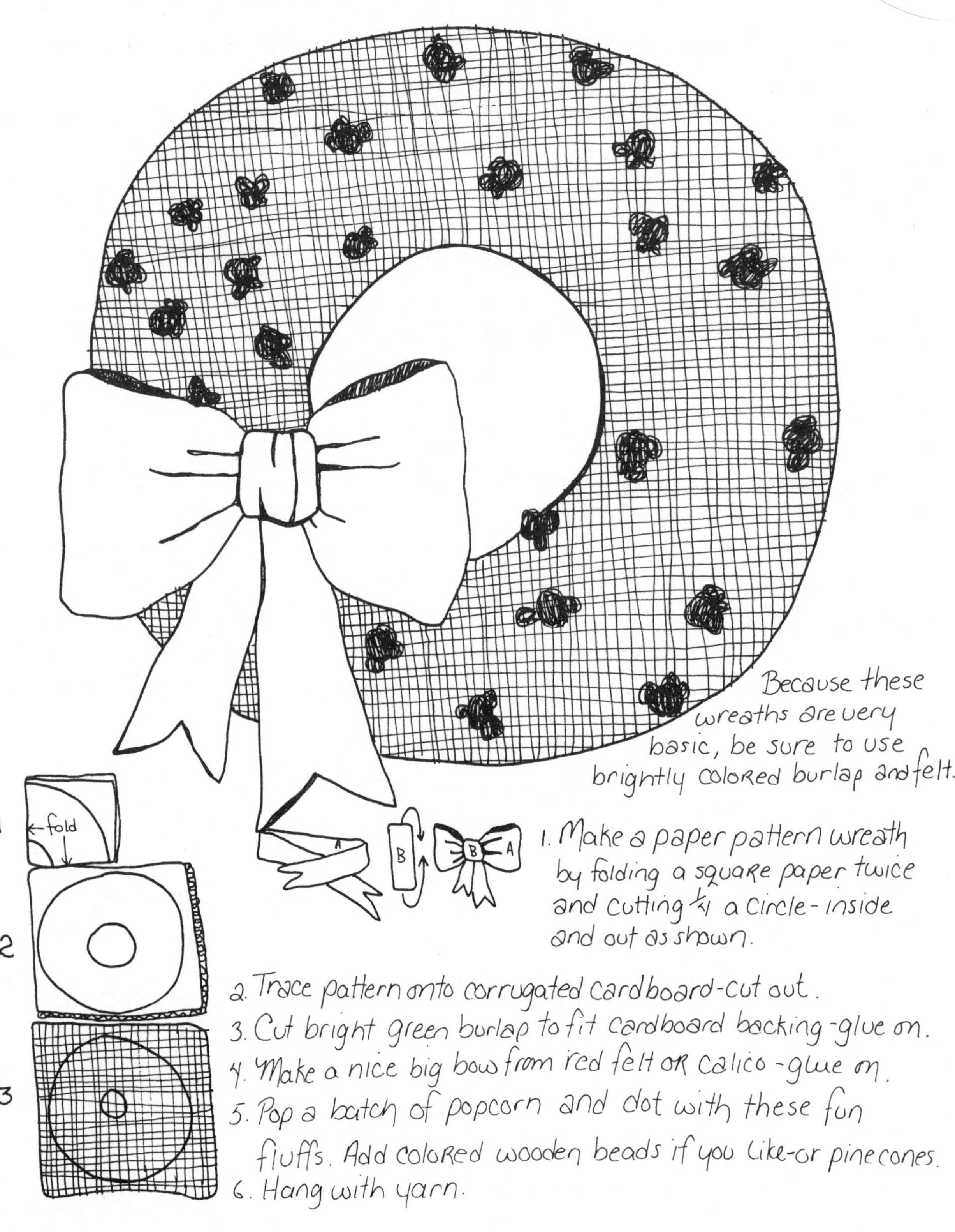

Because these wreaths are very basic, be sure to use brightly colored burlap and felt.

1. Make a paper pattern wreath by folding a square paper twice and cutting 1/4 a circle - inside and out as shown.
2. Trace pattern onto corrugated cardboard-cut out.
3. Cut bright green burlap to fit cardboard backing-glue on.
4. Make a nice big bow from red felt or calico-glue on.
5. Pop a batch of popcorn and dot with these fun fluffs. Add colored wooden beads if you like-or pine cones.
6. Hang with yarn.

BIRDS BIRDS BIRDS

Hang these birdies over your spider plant.

Both birds are made from cardboard and decorated with glued-on stars, silk ties, and print cloth tummies. Make legs from pipe cleaners. Two types of wings are shown. One folds over top of bird; the other slides into a slit in the bird's body.

Add real feathers in the tail and a beaded eyeball.

MORE BIRDS

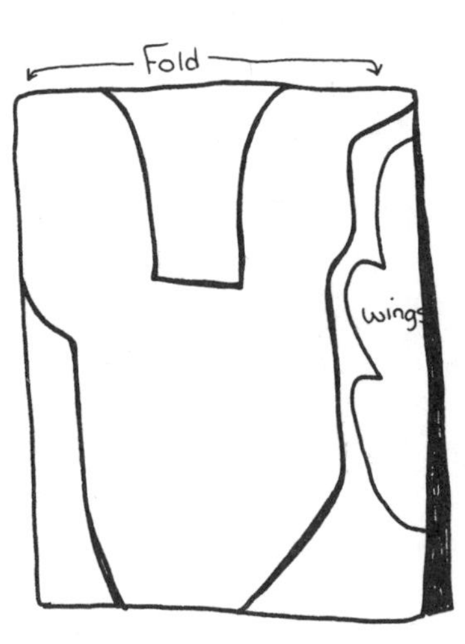

- ★ Dress up birds to look like people you know!
- ★ Make birds holding a prop - umbrella, worms, etc.
- ★ Use them at parties for name place cards.

- ★ make a family "bird" tree.

Use oaktag, shirt cardboard or construction paper. Decorate with yarn, ribbon, beads, feathers, scraps of assorted types of paper - metallic, tissue, construction, etc.

gentle friends

eagle masks

Eagles, Eagles, Eagles! These stately birds were basic to American Indian ceremonial rituals. They represent bravery. Each feather symbolizes power.

1. Fold watercolor paper and draw mask – slit nose, cut out eyes.
2. Using **felt-tipped pen**, design a pattern suggestive of the feather.
3. Add a few beads, yarn and raffia for effect.

slit and staple

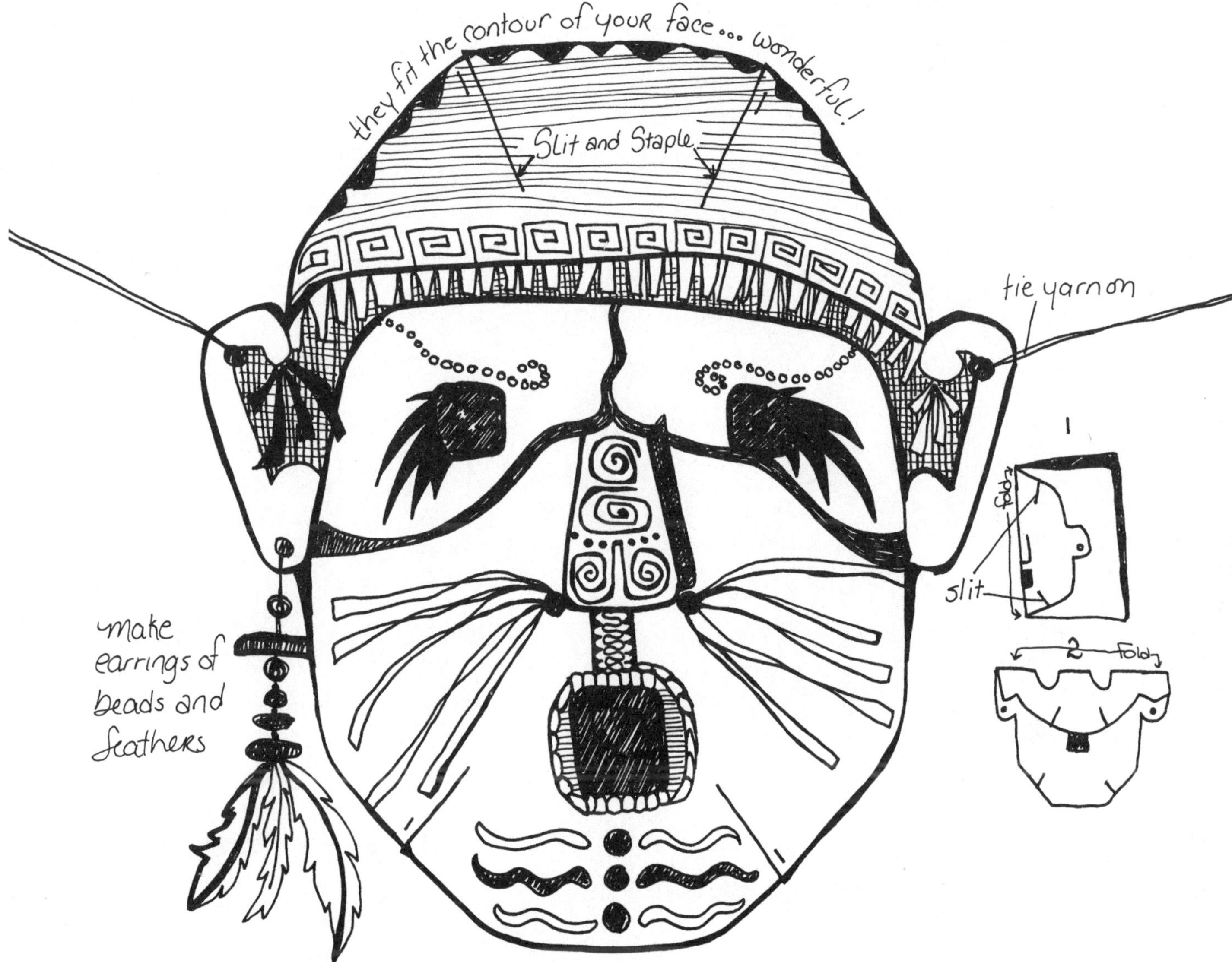

1. Fold a 9" by 12" sheet of watercolor paper in half. Draw ½ of face. Cut out mouth enclosure and part of nose - see #1. Cut mask and slit
2. Fold top of mask downward and cut out eyes. Punch holes in ears.
3. Divide mask into sections. Markers give a really nice textured effect on watercolor paper - color your mask a mood!
4. Staple mask at slits, forming a contoured form. Embellish with scraps!

Movable Mouth

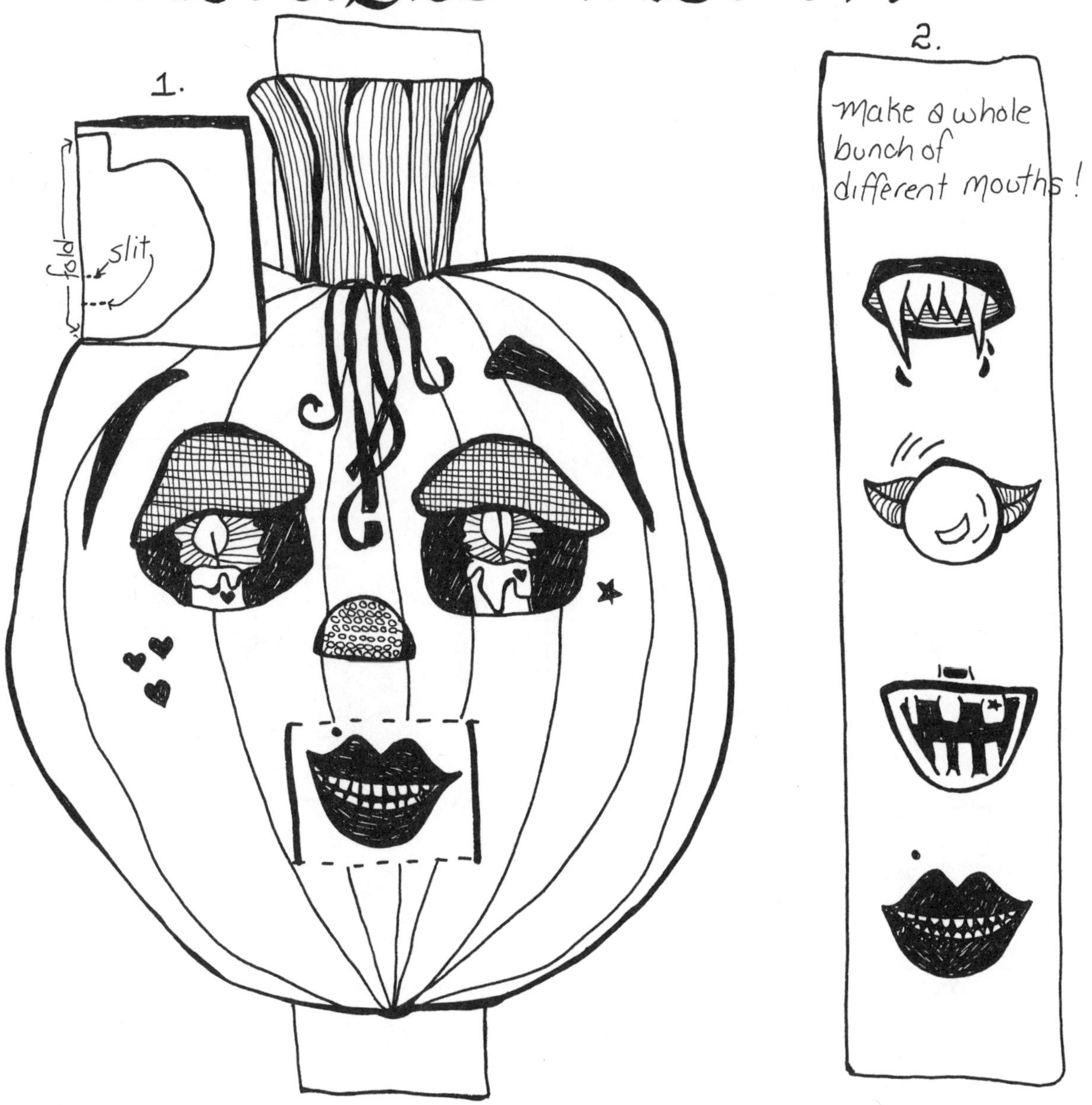

What's in a mouth? Lots of stuff such as teeth, a tongue, tonsils, cavities, fillings, bubble gum, hamburgers, toothpicks and sour balls, and all these are surrounded by changing lips!

1. Fold paper in half, draw head and slit mouth opening - cut out.
2. Cut a strip of paper to weave into mouth slits and draw mouths.
3. Embellish face with scraps. Insert mouth strip.

gliders

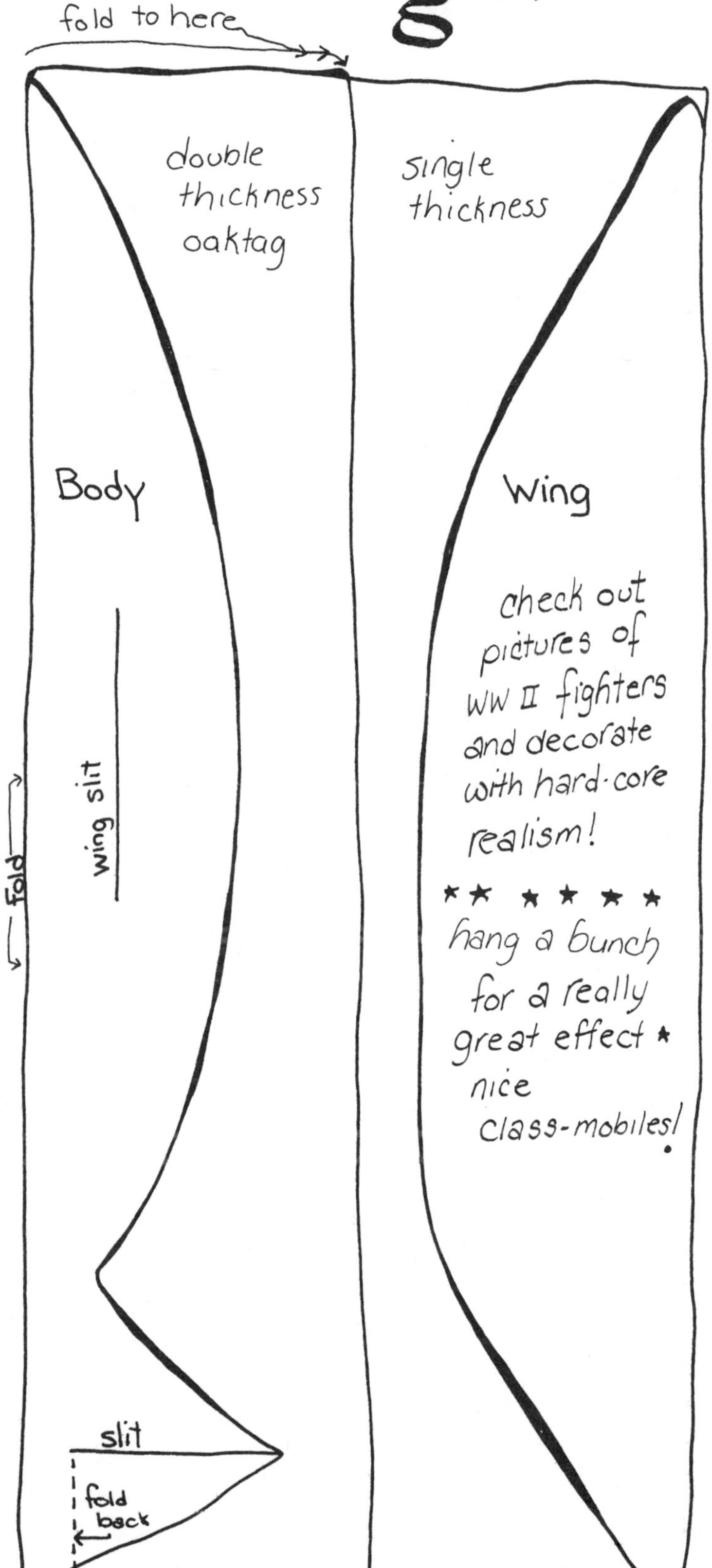

fold to here
double thickness oaktag
single thickness
Body
Wing
wing slit
Fold
slit
fold back
check out pictures of WW II fighters and decorate with hard-core realism!
★★ ★★★★
hang a bunch for a really great effect ★ nice class-mobiles!

make a fierce one!

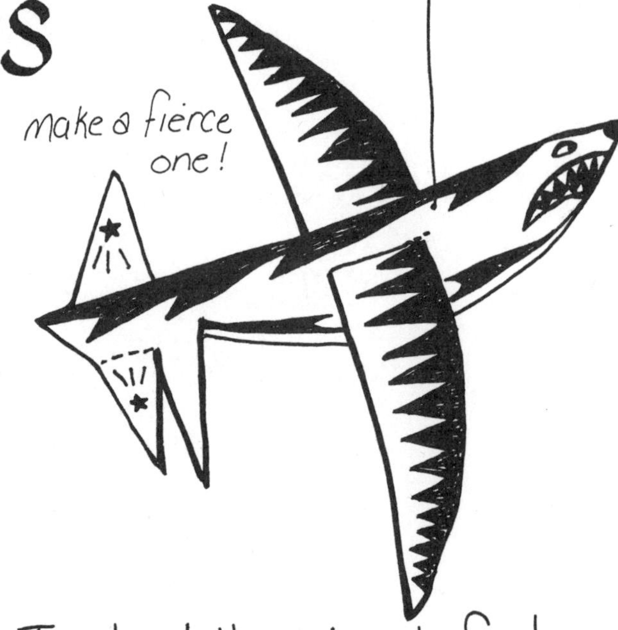

Too bad they don't fly! However they do sway nicely when suspended in an airway.

1. Draw airplane parts as illustrated.
   - body is half-drawn on folded section of oaktag, wing is on single thickness. Cut out.
2. Make wing slits and tail slits. fold back end tail.
3. With markers, bring your glider to life with a character portrayal - Jaws in flight, the mean green, fighting machine.
   - tie wings in with body design.
4. Slide in wing; tie with yarn.

Flying Bats

1. Fold 12" by 18" black construction paper in half. Draw ½ of bat's body, starting and ending on fold - cut out.
2. Color costume with oil pastels.
3. Tape thin, 18" dowel to back of bat.
4. Glue long black paper - tissue or crepe - streamers to bottom tips of wings. (Crepe paper works best!)
5. Add pipe cleaner antenna.

Message Hearts

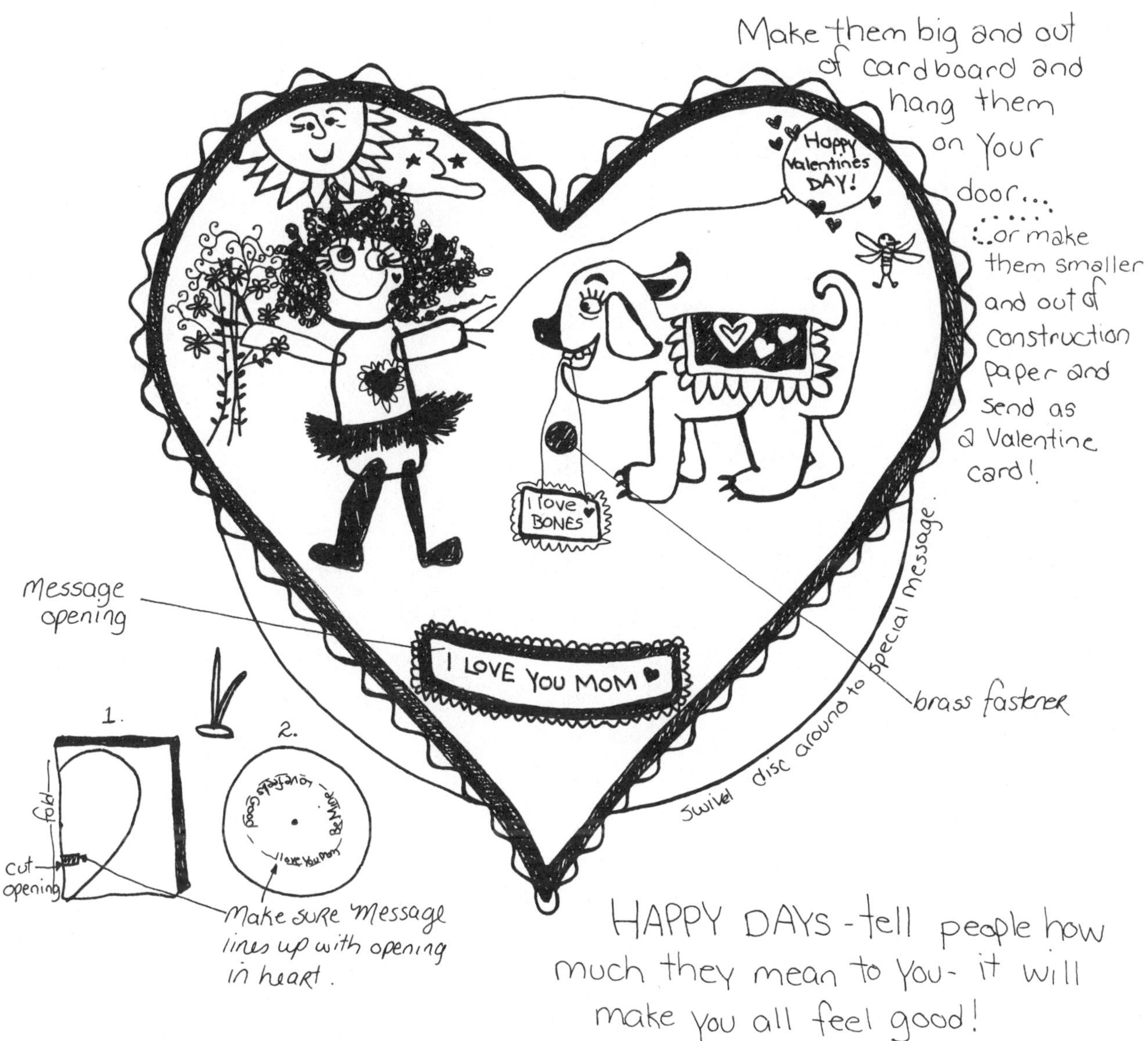

HAPPY DAYS - tell people how much they mean to you - it will make you all feel good!

1. Fold a piece of red construction paper or oaktag in half and cut out a heart - on the fold. Decorate the front. Cut out opening.
2. Cut a white circle and write your messages so that they will fit into the opening after it's fastened.
3. Insert brass fastener through heart and center of message circle.

SANDWICH MONSTERS

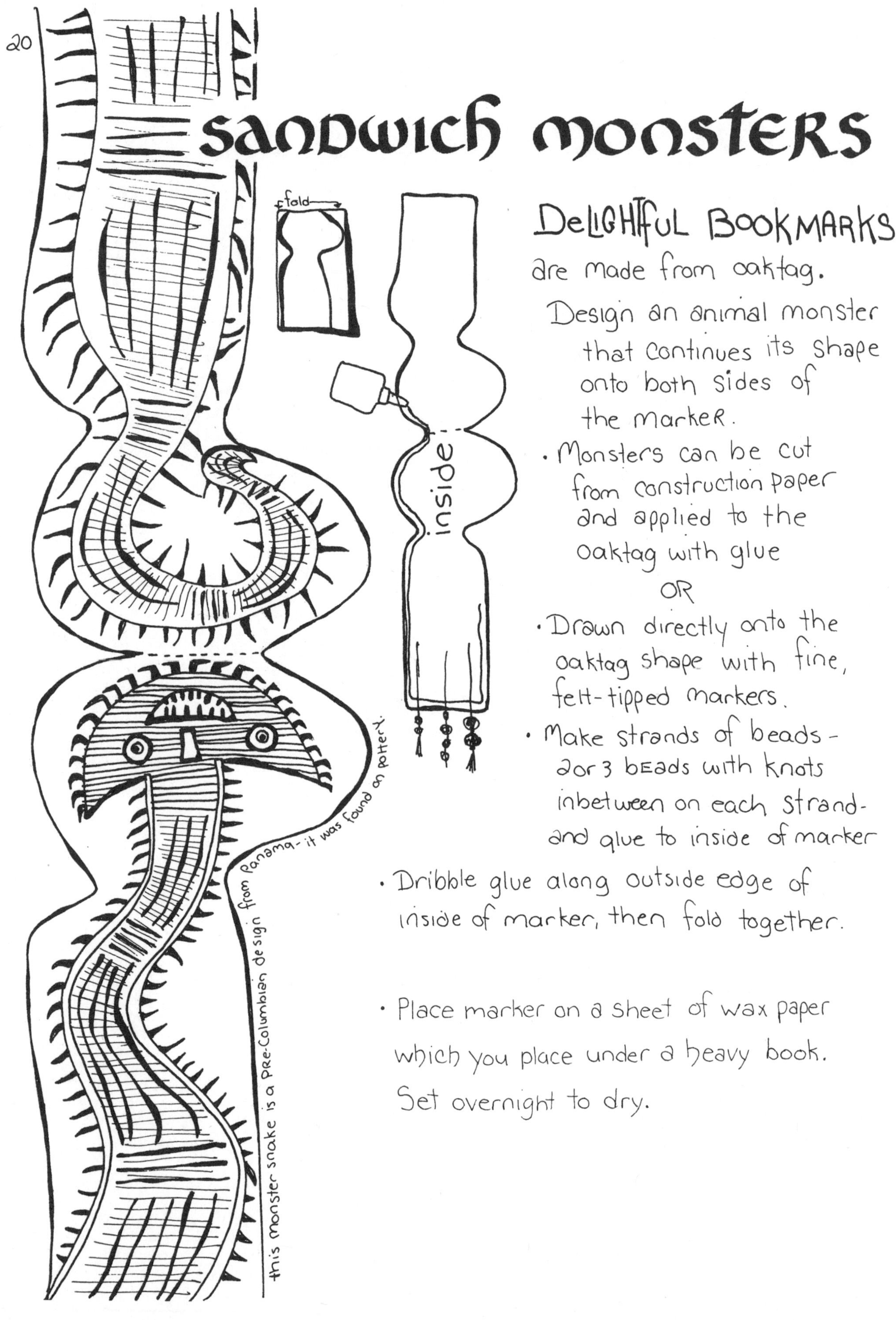

this monster snake is a Pre-Columbian design from Panama- it was found on pottery.

DELIGHTFUL BOOKMARKS

are made from oaktag.

Design an animal monster that continues its shape onto both sides of the marker.

- Monsters can be cut from construction paper and applied to the oaktag with glue

OR

- Drawn directly onto the oaktag shape with fine, felt-tipped markers.
- Make strands of beads - 2 or 3 beads with knots inbetween on each strand- and glue to inside of marker
- Dribble glue along outside edge of inside of marker, then fold together.
- Place marker on a sheet of wax paper which you place under a heavy book. Set overnight to dry.

what's in the cabinet?

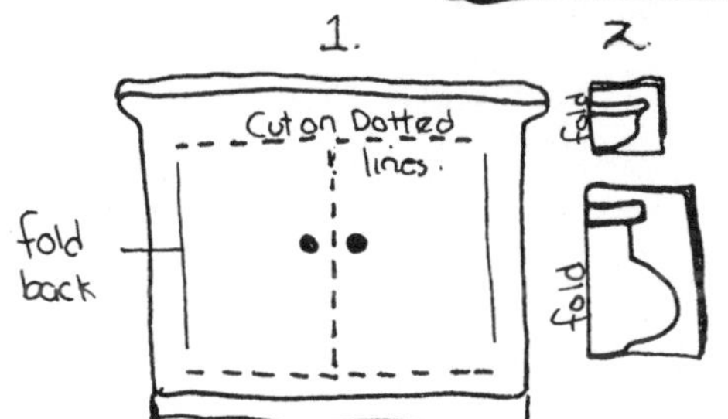

Symmetry - correspondence in size, shape, and position of parts that are on opposite sides of a dividing line or center.
an arrangement marked by regularity and balanced proportions.
Merriam-Webster

THIS IS A GREAT WAY TO EXECUTE SYMMETRY.

The cabinet shown here is rather conventional - typical kitchen stuff - add an element of surprise ~ it's always more fun!

1. Make your cabinet doors by cutting an "I" shape on oaktag. fold back doors and glue frame to another color background paper.
2. Divide into shelf areas with strips of construction paper - or, draw the sections in.
3. The creative stuff comes in here - in loading the shelves with surprise (UN) conventional symmetrical items. Cut each item on the fold of a folded rectangle. Color in patterns and labels and glue on shelves.

INTERIORS

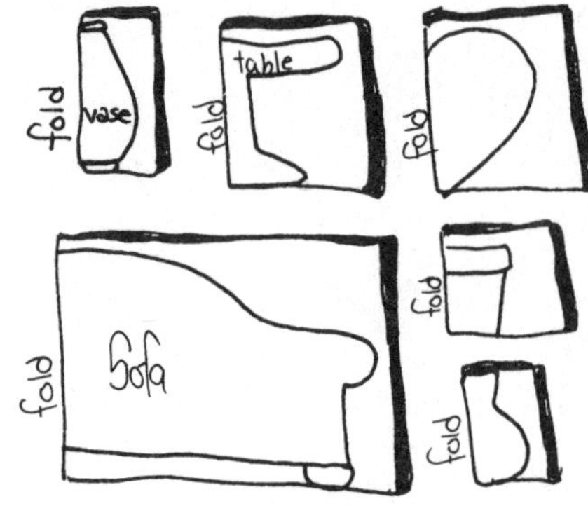

OK—now let's hit on an entire room composed of all symmetrical items made by folding paper in half, drawing half an item on the fold, and cutting it out. Everything, from sofas to plants, may be done through the old fold-and-cut routine. After all your room pieces are glued down, apply decorative motifs on pillows, vases, pictures, books and on and on and on!

Fine-tipped black markers are very effective against construction paper shapes. Add bits of real fabric for collage-type effect.

DESIGN YOUR IMAGINARY RETREAT.

Make one thing completely out of place.

tissue Reliefs

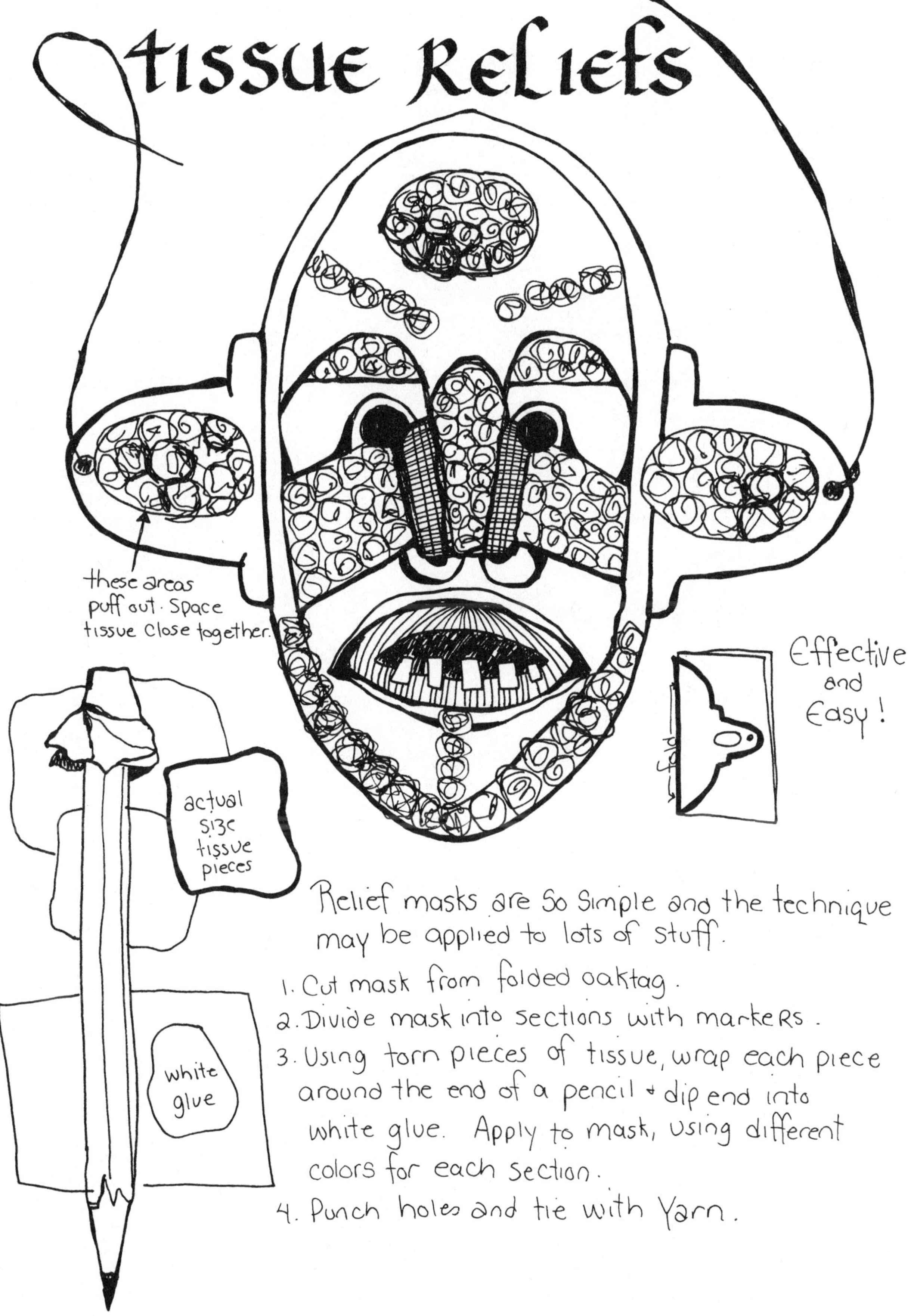

Relief masks are so simple and the technique may be applied to lots of stuff.

1. Cut mask from folded oaktag.
2. Divide mask into sections with markers.
3. Using torn pieces of tissue, wrap each piece around the end of a pencil + dip end into white glue. Apply to mask, using different colors for each section.
4. Punch holes and tie with Yarn.

Fruit Rings

Cut a donut from corrugated cardboard and punch holes on top for hanging. Fold lots of pieces of construction paper in half and make any symmetrical fruit you can think of - oranges, pears, bananas, apples, cherries, peaches, etc. Make stems and leaves and glue on fruit. glue fruit to ring, overlapping for visual effect.

Variation: beautiful stuffed felt fruit wreaths are simple, but more time consuming. Make 2 of each fruit, stitch around sides (leave opening for stuffing), stuff, and close.

MASQUERADING EYES

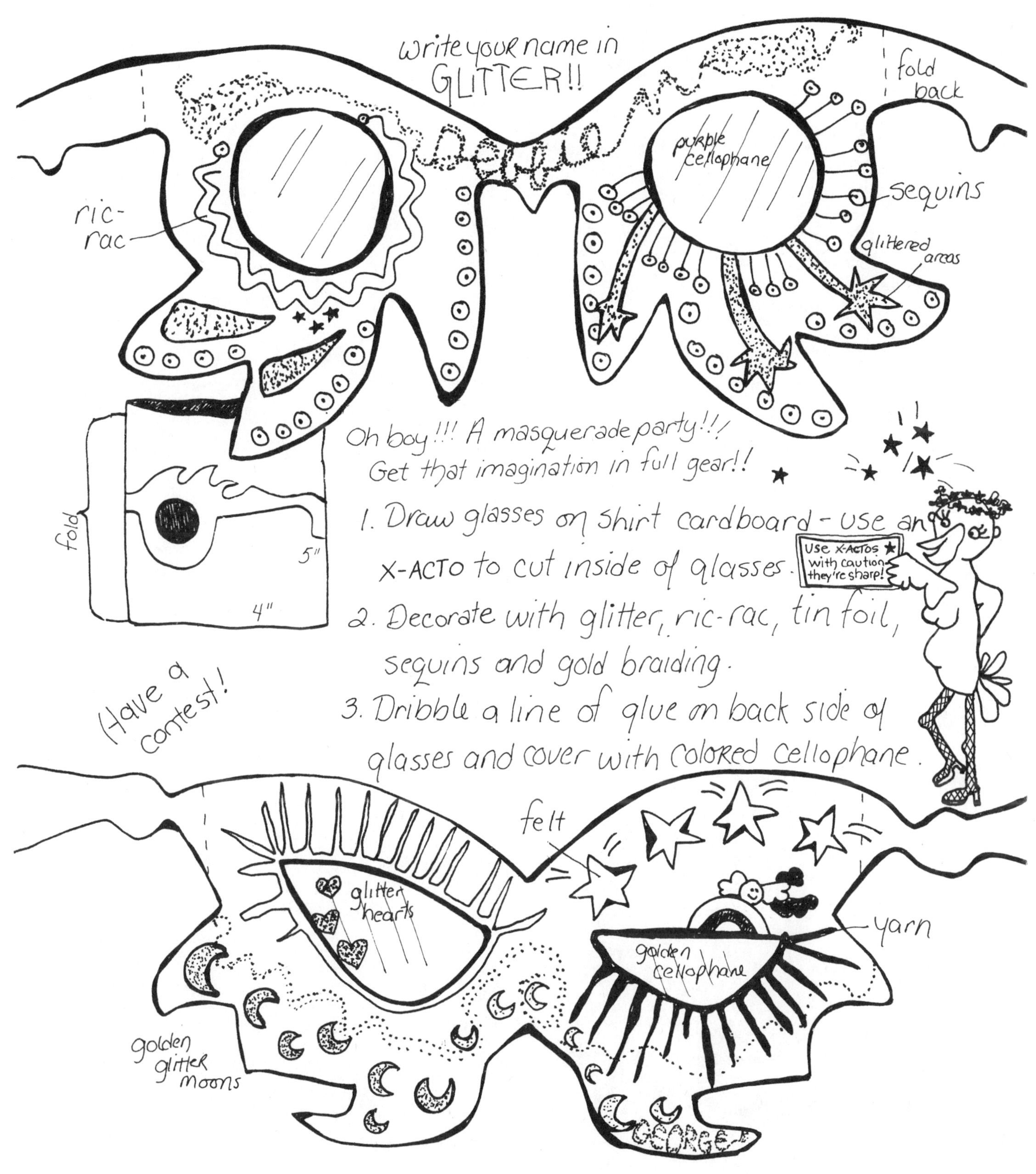

tin plate ornaments

Cone Characters

Cone Characters are a great way to experiment with the endless possibilities of paper. Fold a circle in half and cut along fold- experiment with notching for textural effects or design on ½ circle. Bring straight ends together to form a cone and staple. Attach heads, wings and feathers. Curl strips of construction paper around a pencil or fringe it. Use different combinations of paper- foil, tissue, construction, etc.

cylinder folk

slit and fold back

←fringe

head taped to inside of cylinder

All cylinder characters are formed by making a cylinder from a rectangular piece of paper, stapled along the seam. Construction paper faces, arms and legs are glued to surface of tube. 3-D effects can be achieved by folding, curling strips around a pencil or fringing. Use cotton for beards and muffs.

Bouncing animals

STRETCHING paper

fold fold fold fold fold slits
1 2 3 4
5

Top a bouncing body with your favorite head! Here's how all your bodies are made:

1. Fold a 9" by 12" piece of construction paper lengthwise.
2. Open and fold both edges in toward center.
3. Fold in half.
4. Cut across from one folded edge almost to the other folded edge - alternate cutting from right-folded edge to left-folded edge - all the way to the bottom. Open up and you've got your springing body!
5. Cut out doubles of arms and legs.

'Now make a glorious head for your hoppin' friend - oil pastels decorate nicely. Felt is great for accent - try toenails and bracelets!

CERAMICS

Aaghh.... clay - soft squeezy, fun stuff Earthen treasure! Take a while to squeeze it between your fingers - roll it into meatballs and sausages and worms. Stick your fingers in it, press objects on it, flatten it into a pancake with your palms. Become acquainted with Mother Nature's gift!

Tidbits on water-based clay:

1. Clay needs to be fired (baked) in a kiln (oven) for 6-12 hours to 1800-2300° Fahrenheit to harden it permanently. Pieces should be fired slowly. (A pyrometric cone or pyrometer on the kiln signals maturity.)
2. Before firing, it goes through various stages of drying. It must be completely dry - bone dry - before firing. At any stage, unfired clay can be re-constituted by breaking it up and soaking it in water.
3. If clay dries out too much while you're working with it, it will crack - just add water.
4. Clay must be wedged (or kneaded) to remove air bubbles. Do this before beginning any clay project. Wedge clay by slamming it down hard about twenty times.
5. Any pieces of clay that are joined together must be of the same consistency or they won't hold.
6. Wrap piece in thin plastic if you want to work on it at another time. Even finished projects should dry slowly, so wrap them loosely with plastic too.

7. When joining two pieces of clay together, scratch the surface of each piece, brush on water and fuse, smoothing joint with finger.
8. Carving or designing works best on clay that is leather-hard. It is stiff and will carve very nicely.
9. If you don't have a kiln, pieces may be painted and shellacked over. These pieces will not be as durable as the fired ones, nor can they be used to hold liquid.
10. Glaze may be applied to bisque fired work-work which has been fired once. Glaze gives color and coats pieces with a film which allows for liquid retention.
11. Work over newspaper or the cloth side of oil cloth.

Basic Tools - find them around the house - knives, forks, spoons, awls, screening, wooden nail sticks, stuff to make impressions - nuts, bolts, etc., rolling pins and plastic containers. Loop ceramic tools are very handy.

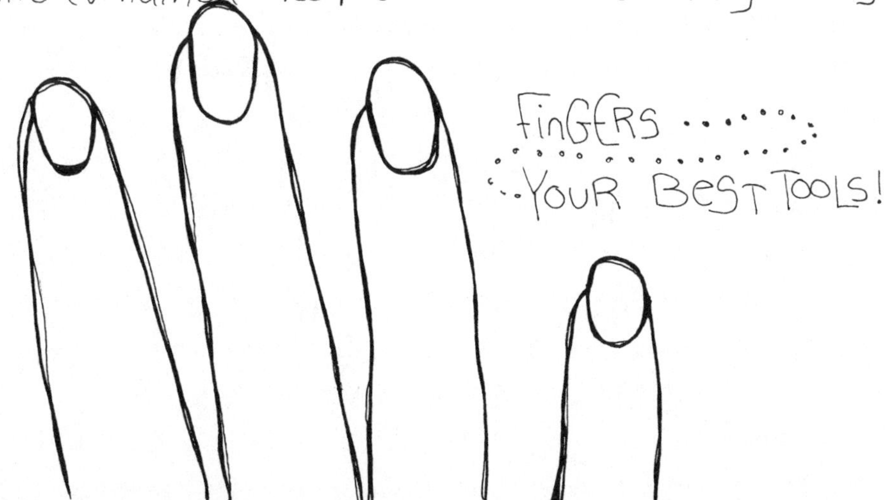

pinch pots

the basic pinch pot— a simple introduction to clay. Roll clay into a ball. Stick both thumbs into center of clay with fingers on outside and gently press thumbs against sides—do this rotating the ball until you have a little clay pot—the walls (sides) shouldn't be over ½" thick. Cute for cactus.

Decorative things to apply on pots:

OOO - little balls

- clay worms

□□□□ - chopped worm.

Decorative things to press into clay:

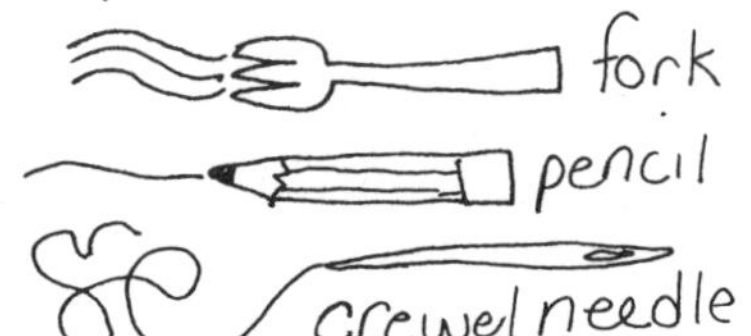

Use small coils - top, bottom, sides. Keep turning pot so you can see how it looks from all sides

experiment with different decorative methods. Be sure to SCORE both pieces of FORM before joining - i.e., a handle should be scored where it will stick to pot. Pot is scored in the same area

Use small balls of clay

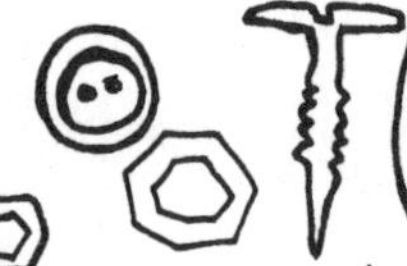

press in objects

scratch in designs

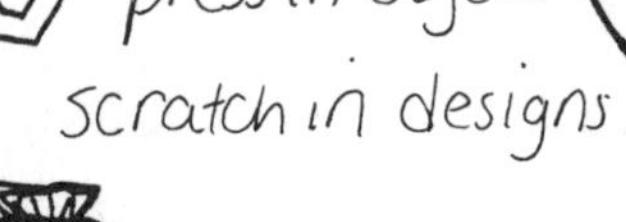

Pinch pot creatures

Create delightfully animated animal pots by starting with the basic pinch pot, then adhering heads, tails, wings, arms and legs. The top two birds have one pot forming the main body; the bottom two consist of 2 pots each - inverted one forms the head. ★ HAVE FUN! ★ Paint with acrylics after fired.

COIL CONSTRUCTION

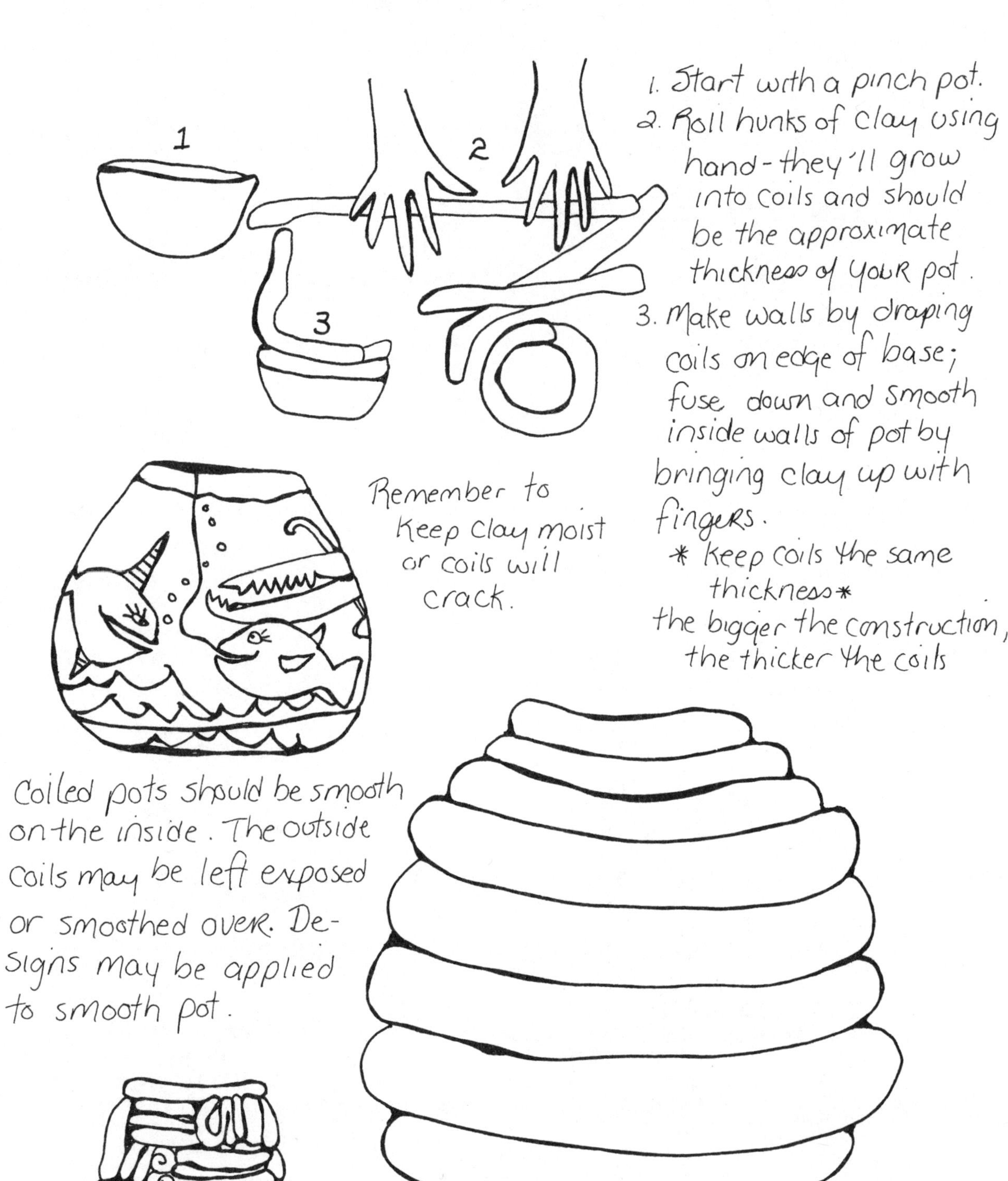

1. Start with a pinch pot.
2. Roll hunks of clay using hand - they'll grow into coils and should be the approximate thickness of your pot.
3. Make walls by draping coils on edge of base; fuse down and smooth inside walls of pot by bringing clay up with fingers.

* Keep coils the same thickness *

the bigger the construction, the thicker the coils

Remember to keep clay moist or coils will crack.

Coiled pots should be smooth on the inside. The outside coils may be left exposed or smoothed over. Designs may be applied to smooth pot.

once you get the hang of working with coils, there are endless possibilities offered by the method.

← work the coils vertically and horizontally.

honey pots

Smile Pots ... using the basic coil construction, make the animal's body. Attach arms, legs and wings. The head forms the bottle stop. Create a head with a long neck to fit inside the opening of the body. Make a coil collar midway down the neck to prevent the head from sinking all the way in. Glaze inside and out, making certain no glaze touches areas that rest on kiln. (Don't glaze bottom of pot or stopper.)

Make a series of these - all different sizes and use them as a canister set - make the necks wider, though.

SLAB CONSTRUCTION

tiles or wall plaques - may be hung with rawhide or used as a hotplate

Slab construction is a wonderful method for creation of planters, bowls, and plates. It can be draped over other forms, slung in a hammock-type support or built in a free fashion.

1. After wedging clay, flatten on a piece of oilcloth and roll it out with a rolling pin - try to keep it even so that walls are no more than ½" thick. (they shouldn't go less than ¼" unless your construction is very small.)
2. Using a knife cut out the shape you'll need to work with Remove. Smooth edges.

For Flat ▭ Shapes

3. Make decorative impressions while clay is still at a workable stage.
   - for pressed-in designs, clay may be soft.
   - for drawn-on designs, clay to be leather-hard.

plaster clay stamp

Let's PAUSE here for a moment to consider some decorative devices that can be made from plaster molds. They're a creative trip in themselves and will be well worth the effort it takes to make them, as you begin stamping them all over your work. We'll make paper cup molds.

Mixing Plaster of Paris

1. Fill plastic bowl ½ way with water
2. Pour plaster into water gently until it begins surfacing.
3. Mix with fingers until smooth

Now:

4. Pour mixture quickly into paper cups - fill ½ way. Let set, then peel away cup.

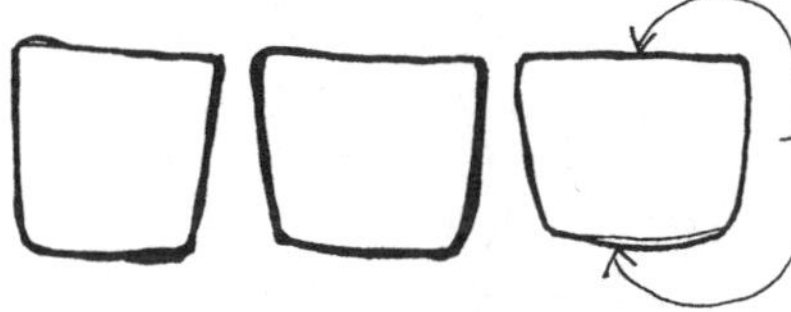

Press Stamps

tops + bottoms can be carved with any sharp tool - make fine lines, or gouge out pockets of plaster - chip away to make a pocket, then smooth rough parts with sandpaper.

Roller Stamps

Remove plaster

Clay

Sides can be carved, then rolled along clay to create borders for plates, pots, etc.

these plaster stamps are great - experiment with them - just press them into a flattened meatball of clay and poke a hole up top and you have a chain pull, or a key holder!

the deeper you carve plaster, the higher the impression you'll get in clay.

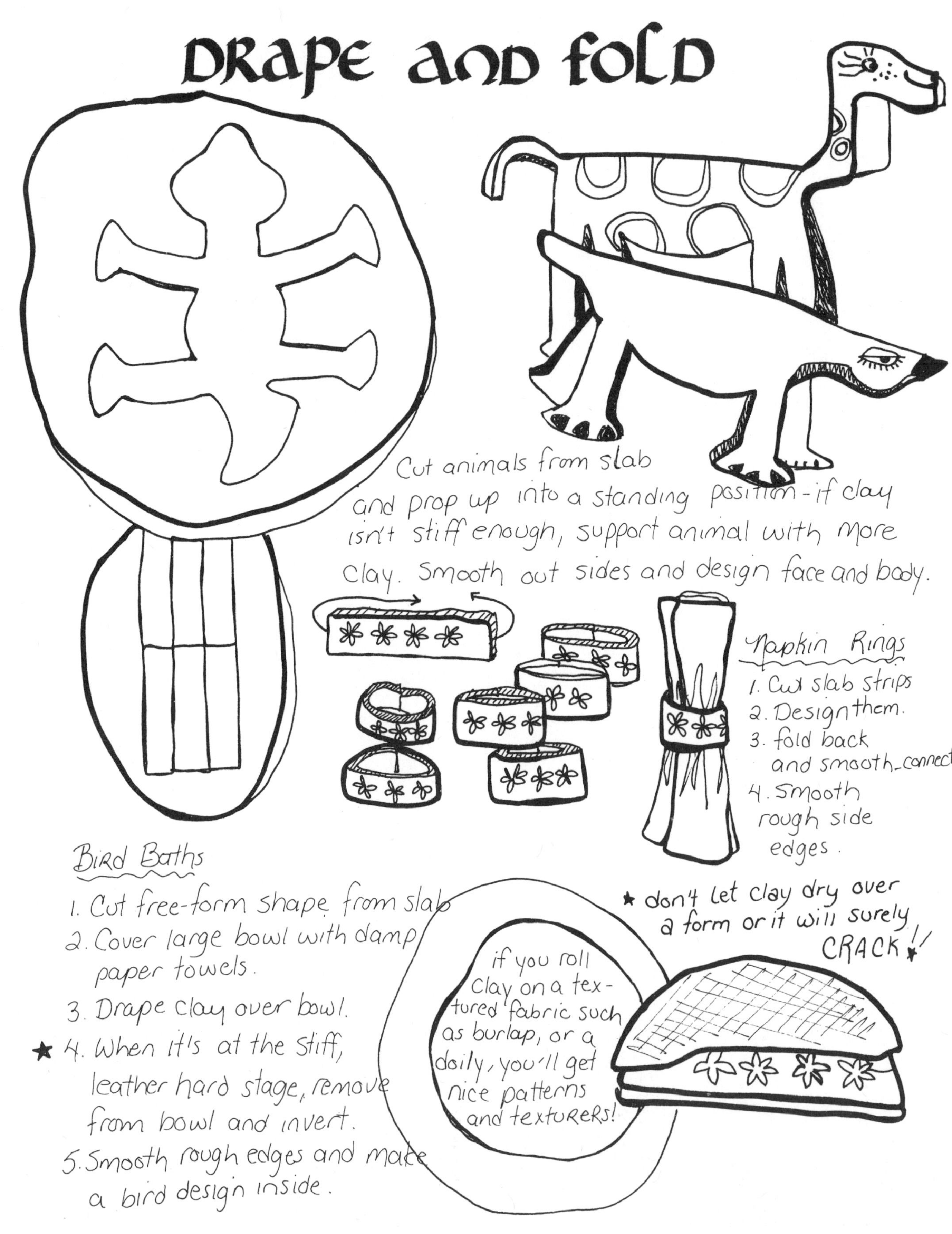
DRAPE AND FOLD
Cut animals from slab and prop up into a standing position - if clay isn't stiff enough, support animal with more clay. Smooth out sides and design face and body.
Napkin Rings
1. Cut slab strips
2. Design them.
3. fold back and smooth_connect.
4. Smooth rough side edges.
Bird Baths
1. Cut free-form shape from slab
2. Cover large bowl with damp paper towels.
3. Drape clay over bowl.
★ 4. When it's at the stiff, leather hard stage, remove from bowl and invert.
5. Smooth rough edges and make a bird design inside.
if you roll clay on a textured fabric such as burlap, or a doily, you'll get nice patterns and texturers!
★ don't let clay dry over a form or it will surely CRACK!!★

WIND CHIMES

Now that we have our plaster stamps, let's get some service from them! Torn clay wind chimes are music to anyone's ears. They're beautiful to look at and dance on your back porch – and they're easy as pie to make! Simply roll a thin slab (¼") of clay over burlap – do both sides. Tear one large piece off top of slab and make two holes. This will be the main support from which you will hang all your other pieces. Next, tear up the other pieces of clay into shapes larger than the circumference of your stamp. Stamp patterns on torn clay pieces. Poke hanging holes in. After pieces are fired, tie together with strong fiber – jute, yarn, etc.

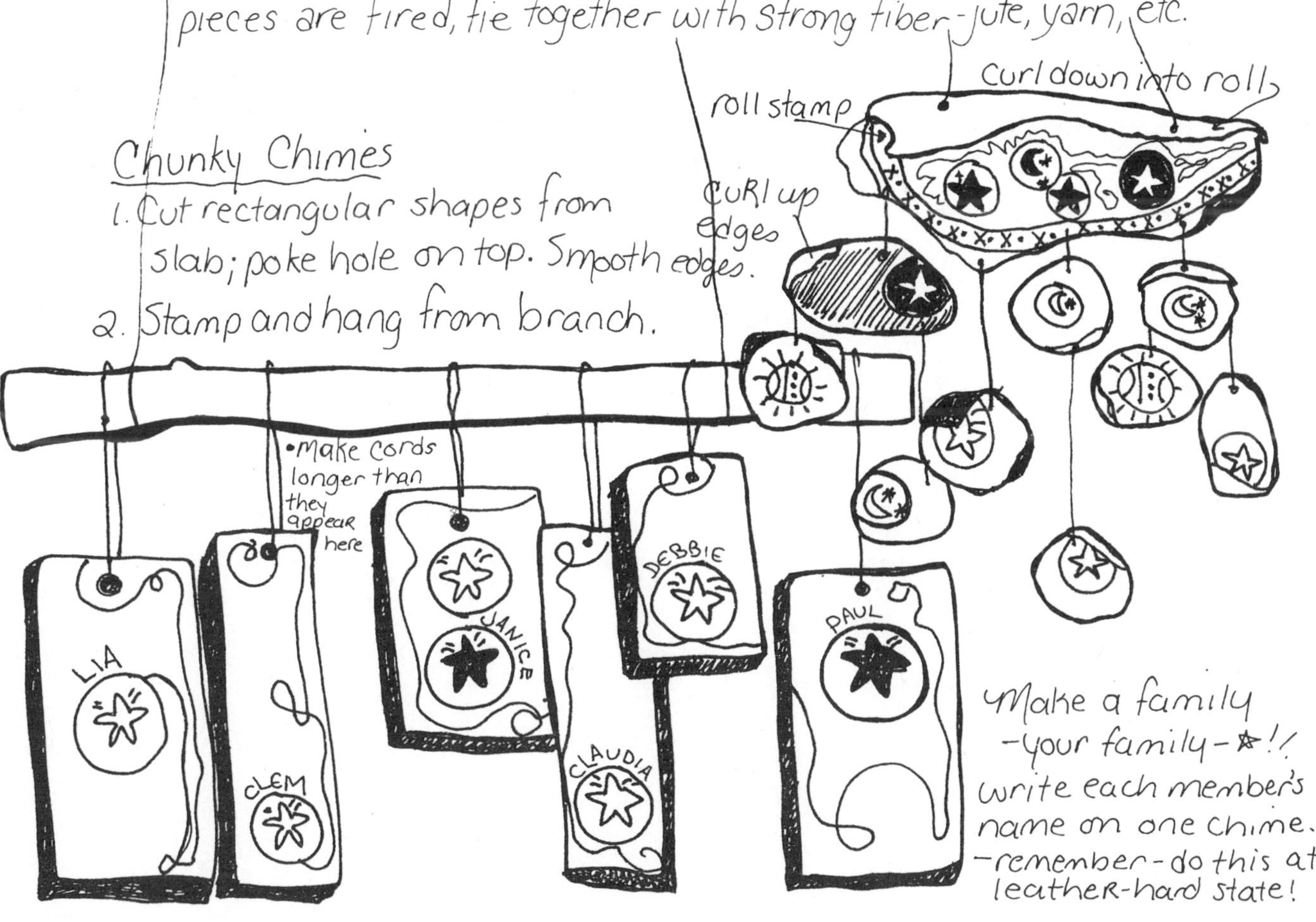

MORE CHIMES

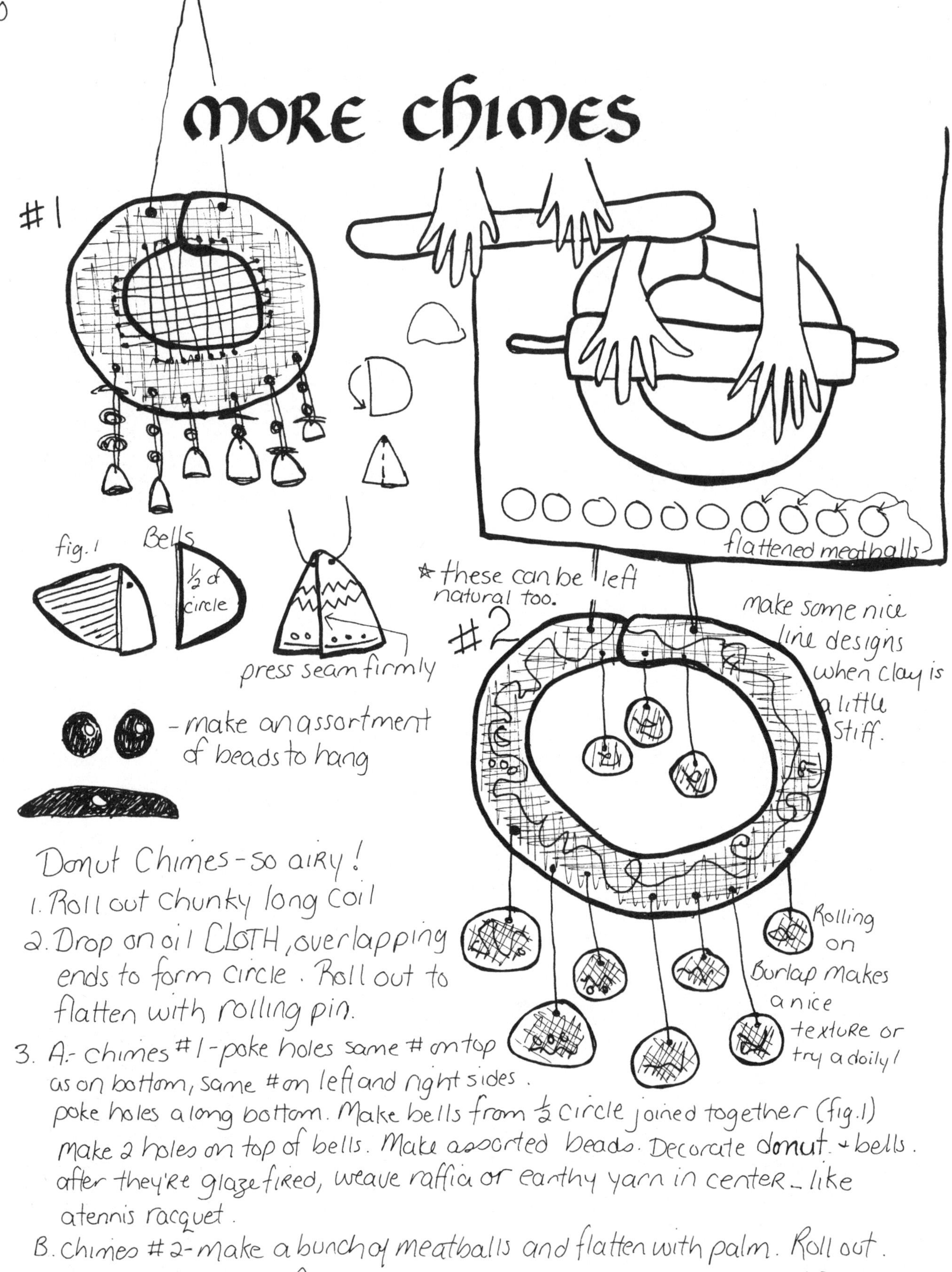

Donut Chimes - so airy!

1. Roll out Chunky long Coil
2. Drop on oil CLOTH, overlapping ends to form circle. Roll out to flatten with rolling pin.
3. A.- chimes #1 - poke holes same # on top as on bottom, same # on left and right sides. poke holes along bottom. Make bells from ½ circle joined together (fig. 1) make 2 holes on top of bells. Make assorted beads. Decorate donut + bells. after they're glaze fired, weave raffia or earthy yarn in center - like a tennis racquet.

   B. chimes #2 - make a bunch of meatballs and flatten with palm. Roll out.
4. Hang bells, beads and flattened meatballs to chimes - consider different elevations for visual pleasure. Shells can be used along with seagull feathers.

Sensational Slab

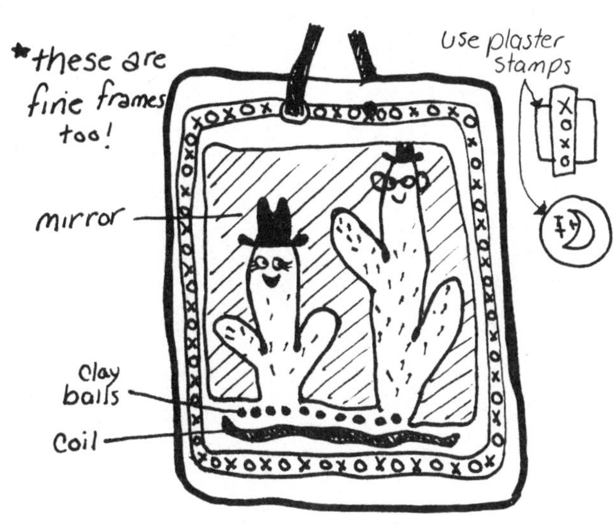

Wonderful mirror frames - make them of a smaller, more decorative nature, as the larger ones tend to warp.

1. Cut a shape from a ½" slab - cut out interior; these may be any shape - if you want the mirror to have more of a function, simply make a frame with a large cut-out center. Poke holes
2. Smooth the edges and carve or stamp designs. Apply small coils.
3. After it's fired, you can achieve a nice burnished effect by rubbing brown shoe polish over it - the polish fills the depressed areas more, giving you a nice effect.
4. Hold mirror to back using heavy duty cloth or plastic tape.
5. Hang with rawhide.

Easy Wall Plaques to Make people feel nice

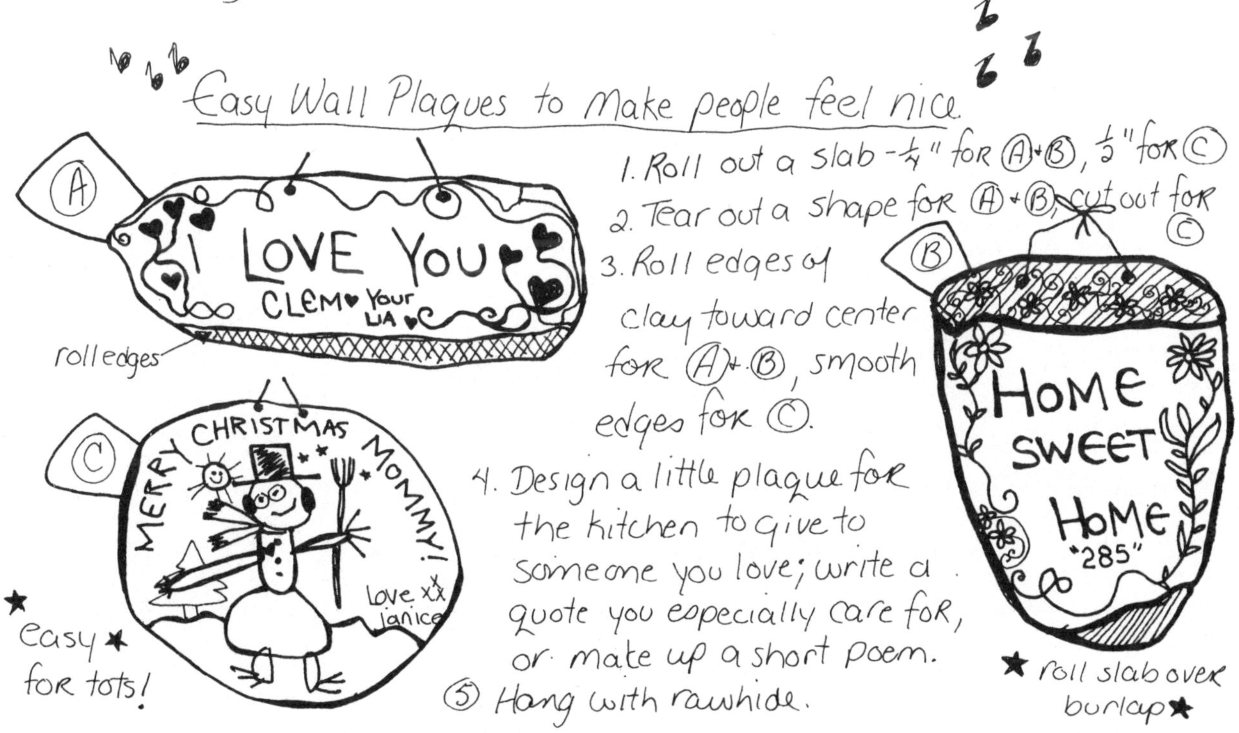

1. Roll out a slab - ¼" for Ⓐ+Ⓑ, ½" for Ⓒ
2. Tear out a shape for Ⓐ+Ⓑ, cut out for Ⓒ
3. Roll edges of clay toward center for Ⓐ+Ⓑ, smooth edges for Ⓒ.
4. Design a little plaque for the kitchen to give to someone you love; write a quote you especially care for, or make up a short poem.
5. Hang with rawhide.

SLAB AND WRAP

Weed holders and plant holders can be made very easily with the fold and wrap method of slab. Simply roll out a slab and...... for a

weed holder (A):

1. Cut a rectangular shape and bring sides together toward center, overlapping 1!" (Insert a rolled up piece of newspaper for support) press down seam with a tool, making a designed impression.
2. Punch 2 holes in back; decorate.

Plant Holder (B):

1. Cut a simple symmetrical shape; crumple newspaper and place it on one half, folding the other half over and pressin sides together with thumb.
2. Smooth edges and decorate
3. Punch back holes.

Multi-Plant Holder (C):

1. Cut one main slab and three smaller ones.
2. Place smaller ones on top of large slab, stuffing a little newspaper in each for support; press in around sides, punch holes.

Slab pots

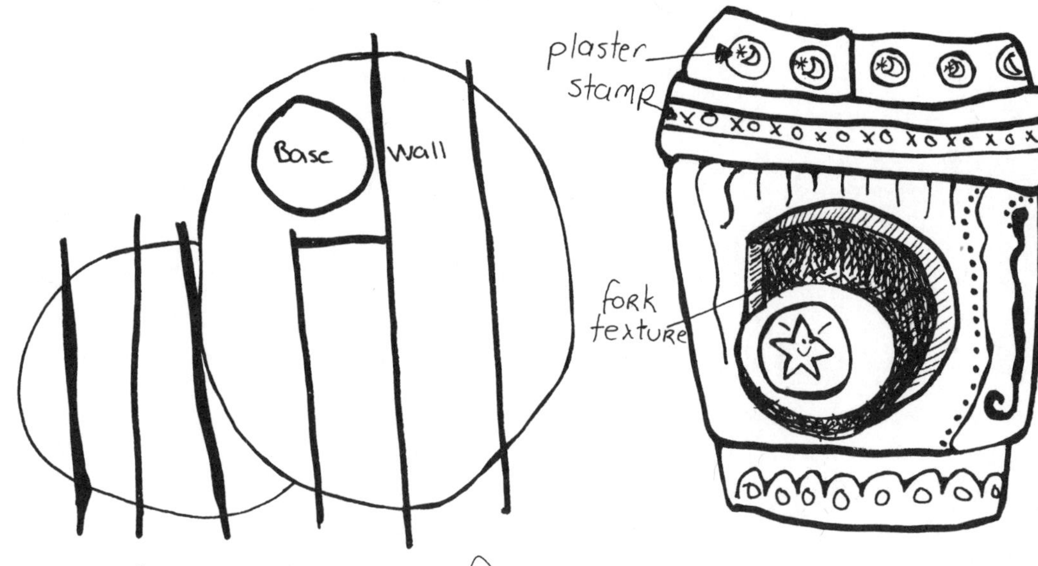

Plastic lazy susans are perfect for putting your pots on while you're working on them.

Slab Pots are much faster to make than coil. Experiment - pots do not have to be symmetrical - they do have to have a pleasing form. Here's how:

1. Cut circle for base and lots of strips to form walls.
2. Wrap strip around base. Be sure you score each part of clay that connects to another part, then smooth over firmly with your finger.
3. You can keep adding more strips for a taller pot - stamp some plaster prints on a strip. When you layer clay, you can overlap it and smooth it on the inside, letting the outside layer show.
4. Press on little coils and balls; design with sharp tool.

animals

Wonderful animals that you can use every day! Simply make a basic coil or slab pot and add heads, wings and tails.

Make beautiful things serviceable!

candle shades

Summer Evenings — so romantic

1. Roll out a slab of clay 1/2" thick.
2. Cut a strip to form a cylinder.
3. Join sides together, overlapping clay 3/4." Smooth seam.
4. Pinch top closed and smooth over.
5. Allow form to stiffen a while, then carve openings into clay - make a mask - carve openings for eyes, nose and mouth. Carve surface tribal markings. Add several coils to base for additional decor.
6. Dry piece a little more, then smooth over rough edges with a stiff finger.
7. Fire and glaze for sparkle!!

COIL BOWLS

damp paper toweling

Coils in A Mold - Perfect!

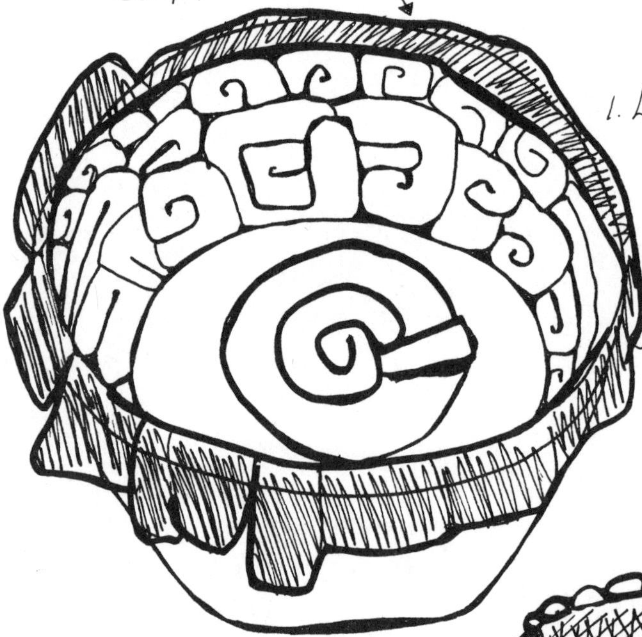

1. Line a rounded bowl with damp paper towels.
2. Lay coils into bowl, starting with bottom center.
3. Work up to side, spiraling, weaving and fitting one shape snuggly beside the next. Fill small spaces with little balls.

smooth inside

4. Smooth entire inside of bowl with your fingers.
5. When clay is stiff enough to hold the shape of the mold, gently remove bowl.
6. The outside of the bowl will be designed with all your coil build-ups.
7. After they are fired, these bowls look really nice with several coats of brown shoe polish - the polish lodges into the cracks, deepening their color.

- make sure you use a bowl that flares outward

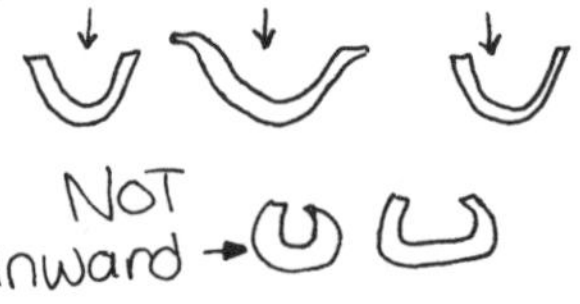

NOT inward

people pots

Once you're familiar with both coil and slab methods of construction, try making a people pot, using the heads of every one you'd want to have at your next party!

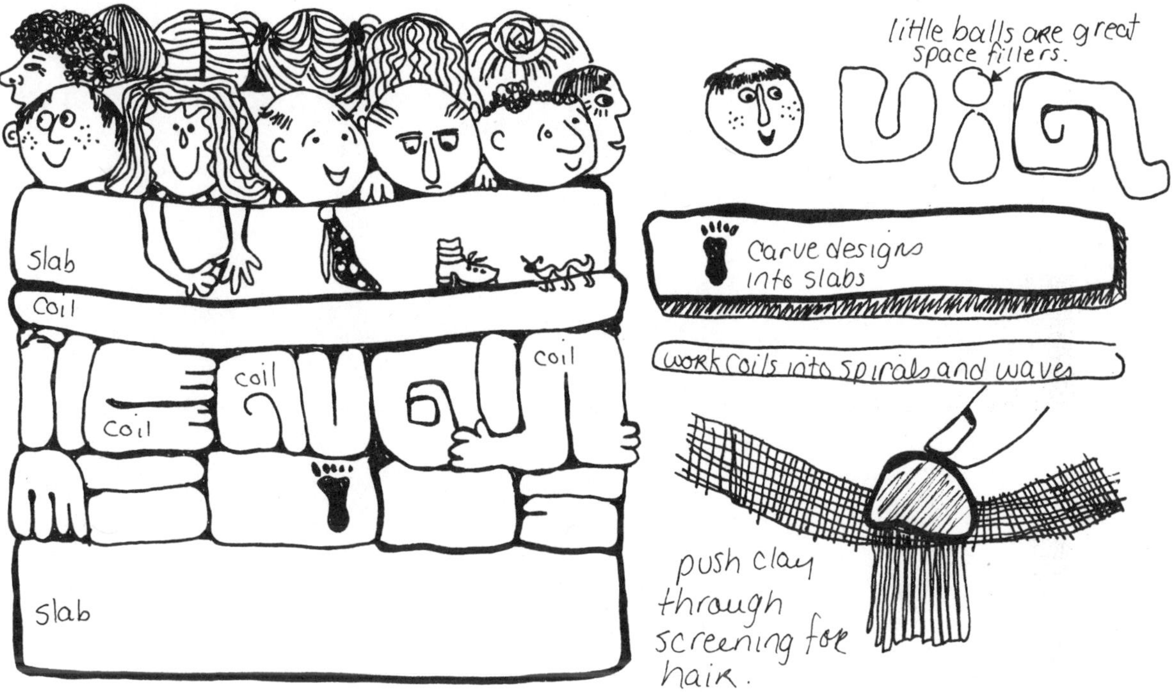

Slabs of clay are intermingled with coils all the way to the top of your pot - leave the outside showing the layered effect, and smooth the inside. Lastly, make balls to turn into heads and line them along the edge of your last layer. Make different facial expressions and hairstyles on each person. Smooth the inside-bottom of the heads together and connect some heads together at the sides. You want a good secure ring of heads or they'll never make the firing. Designs can be engraved on the surface when the clay is stiff.

fast food fantasy

Junk food - aaah - easier on YOUR eyes than in YOUR tummy!

Make an array of your favorites - desserts, Candies or fast food edibles...

Before starting, be SURE YOUR Clay is well wedged as you'll be working in fairly thick proportions. Do not make shapes too thick - the thicker or denser the piece, the greater the chance of explosion in the kiln.

After goodies are fired, they may be painted with enamels or temperas with a coat of shellac.

Why not make a full meal of ceramic non-edibles - from hamburgers to nuts to a hot-fudge Sundae! Yum!

Delightful Dolls

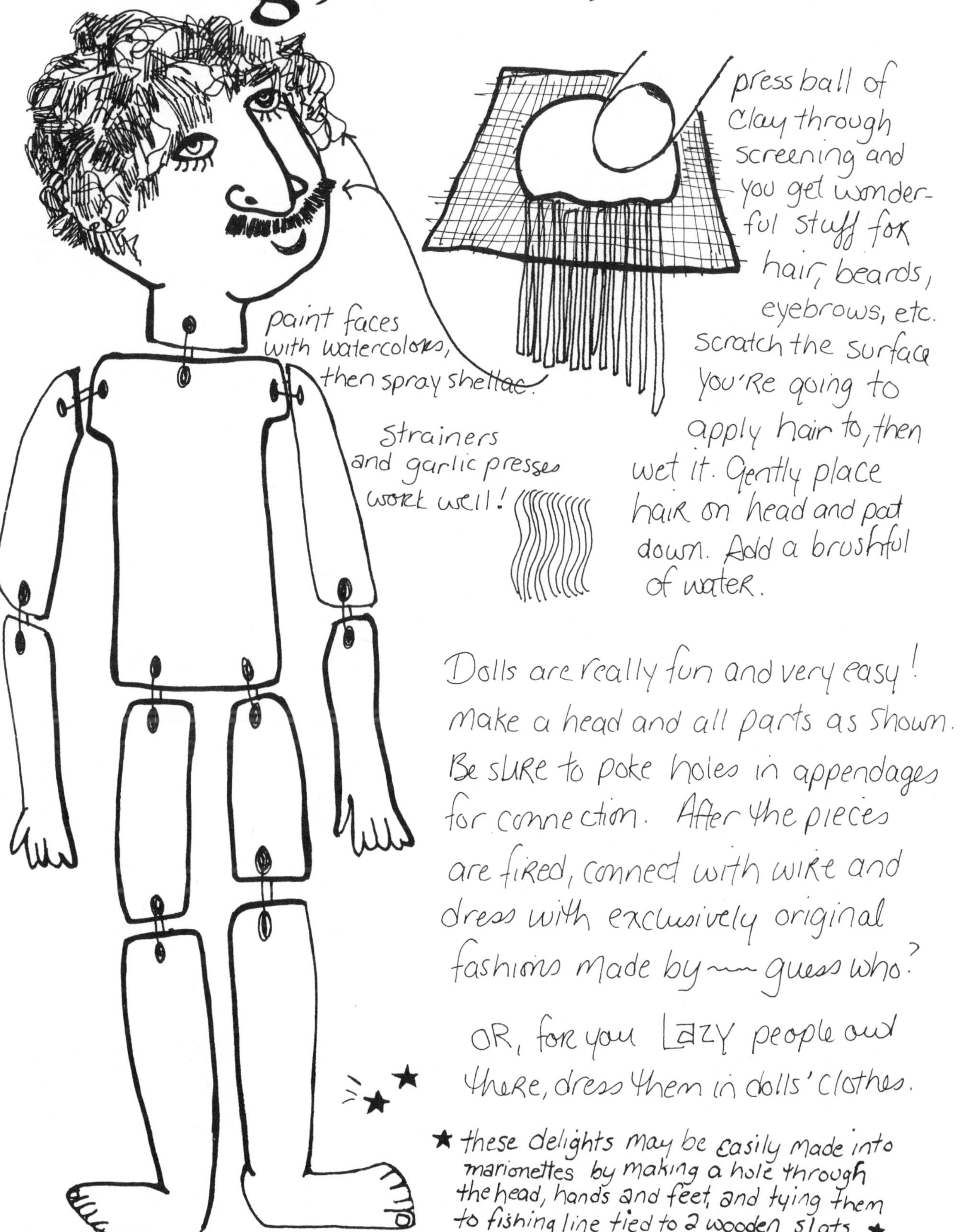

Dolls are really fun and very easy! Make a head and all parts as shown. Be sure to poke holes in appendages for connection. After the pieces are fired, connect with wire and dress with exclusively original fashions made by ~~ guess who?

OR, for you LAZY people out there, dress them in dolls' clothes.

★ these delights may be easily made into marionettes by making a hole through the head, hands and feet, and tying them to fishing line tied to 2 wooden slats. ★

the nativity

A great group project, this scene allows for each child to pick his favorite contribution to the nativity. The people are about 5" tall and easily formed from clay, as are the animals. After firing, paint with watercolors, then spray shellac. Dress with muslin, burlap and jute for ties. Create the wise men's clothes with silks and satin scraps. Yarn hair and fake fur are added to authenticate animals and people. Have 3 kids work on the stable—collect twigs and straw—hammer together main supports or secure together with wire. Roof can be made with corrugated cardboard covered with straw.

glue on pipe cleaner

leaves are 4" long—pipe cleaner allows shape to be bent to form nice curves—after wrapping pipe cleaners around twig, wrap tape around pipe cleaners for additional security.

(remove wrapper of cup & paint plaster)

Palm trees are made by pouring plaster into dixie cups, then inserting a twig. Leaves are made with felt supported by a 6" pipe cleaner running down center vein, with 2" extended. Wrap extended pipe cleaner around twig and glue on acorns for coconuts.

- Make little sacks of treasures for the wise men to hold ★ fill the sacks with real spices!
- cut 2 yellow stars - sandwich in a pipe cleaner and glue sides together - secure into roof of stable.
- scatter straw on ground.

BIRD IN A NEST

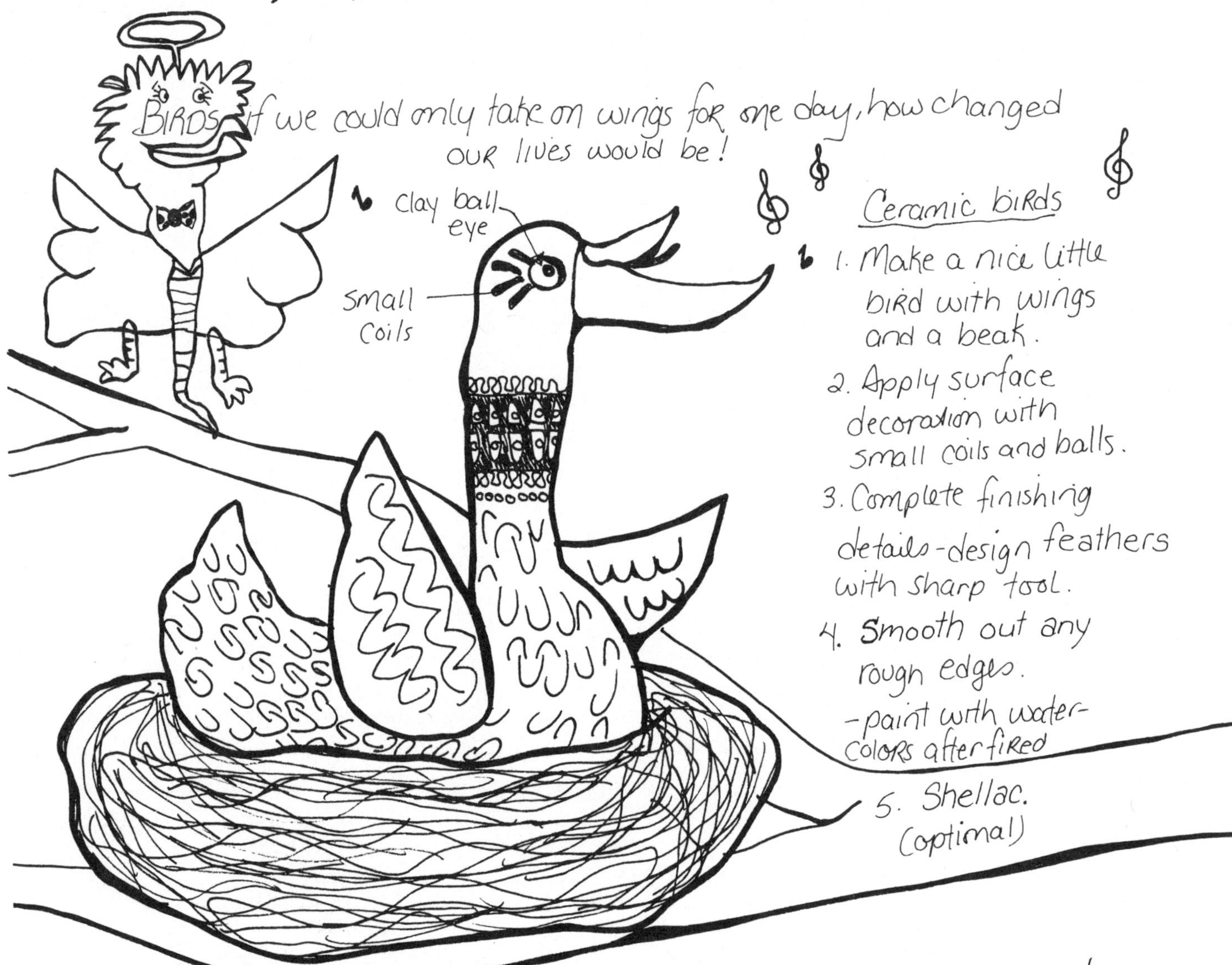

Nests

1. Fray a rectangle of natural colored burlap - about 9" by 12"
2. Dip strands in papier-mâché mixture, squeezing off extra.
3. Create the nest with the strands going in a circular, nest-like fashion - dry on wax paper.

★ When both bird and nest are completed, rest the bird in its new rest area and find a nice dried branch to set your creation on.

★ Make several birds in nests and set them in large house plants!

JEWELRY

Pins, pendants, beads, necklaces, tie-tacs and barrettes can all be made from clay ★ appropriate findings, such as clips for tie-tacks and pin backs, may be glued on after the clay has been fired and painted with enamels. Work with care and patience forming your basic shape, smoothing it around the edges, then roll small coils for decorative images. When clay is at a leather-hard dry stage, carving designs is easiest.

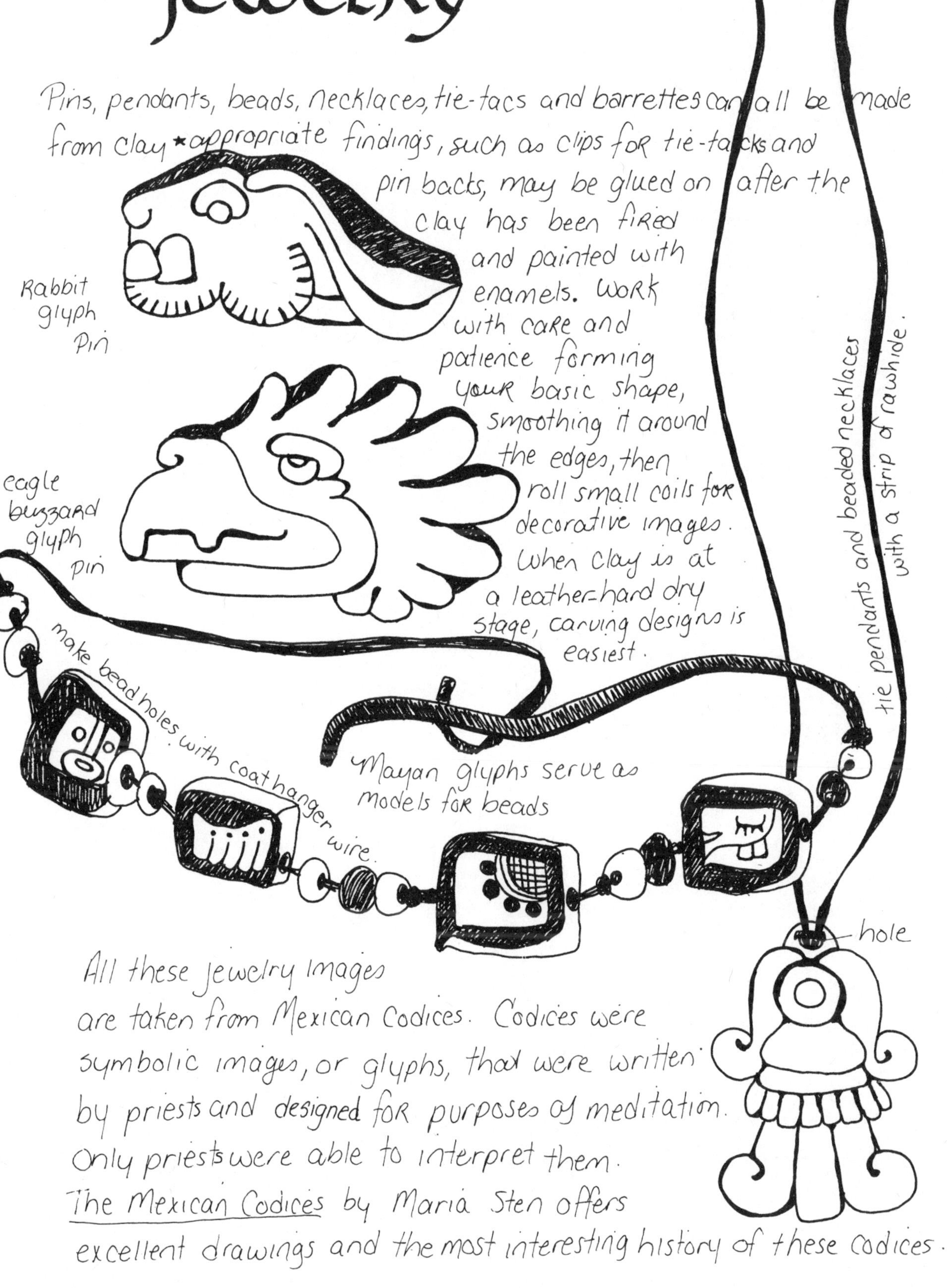

All these jewelry images are taken from Mexican Codices. Codices were symbolic images, or glyphs, that were written by priests and designed for purposes of meditation. Only priests were able to interpret them. The Mexican Codices by Maria Sten offers excellent drawings and the most interesting history of these codices.

Chanukah Creations

oh dreidel dreidel dreidel ★
I made it out of clay ★
Oh dreidel dreidel dreidel ★
oh dreidel I shall play!!!

Insert dowel after fired →

play for nuts!

CAROL JOEL

Clay dreidels are easy to make. Form your dreidel and carve these letters on each side → נ, ג, ה, ש. Push a wooden dowel down on the dreidel and wiggle it around - clay shrinks while drying and during firing, so make hole a little larger while clay is still moist. Paint your dreidels after they're fired. Insert dowel - wrap masking tape around inserted part if it's too loose. Shave some wood off dowel if it's too tight.

Slab and Coil MENORAHS

1. Cut a slab strip ½" thick and drape over an aluminum foil box which has damp paper toweling on the top. Smooth rough edges.

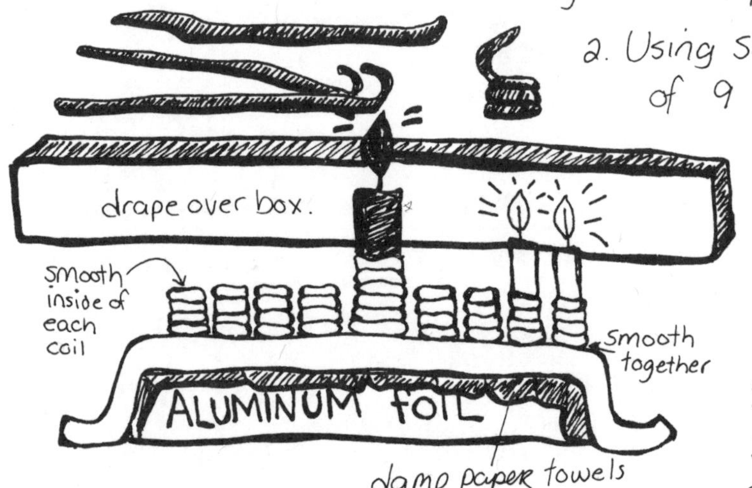

2. Using small coils, make a row of 9 candle-stick holders.
   - start with the center one, making it tallest, then space 4 shorter ones on each side of it. Smooth the insides of each coiled candleholder. Be sure each holder is well secured to slab - smooth down clay from coil to slab.

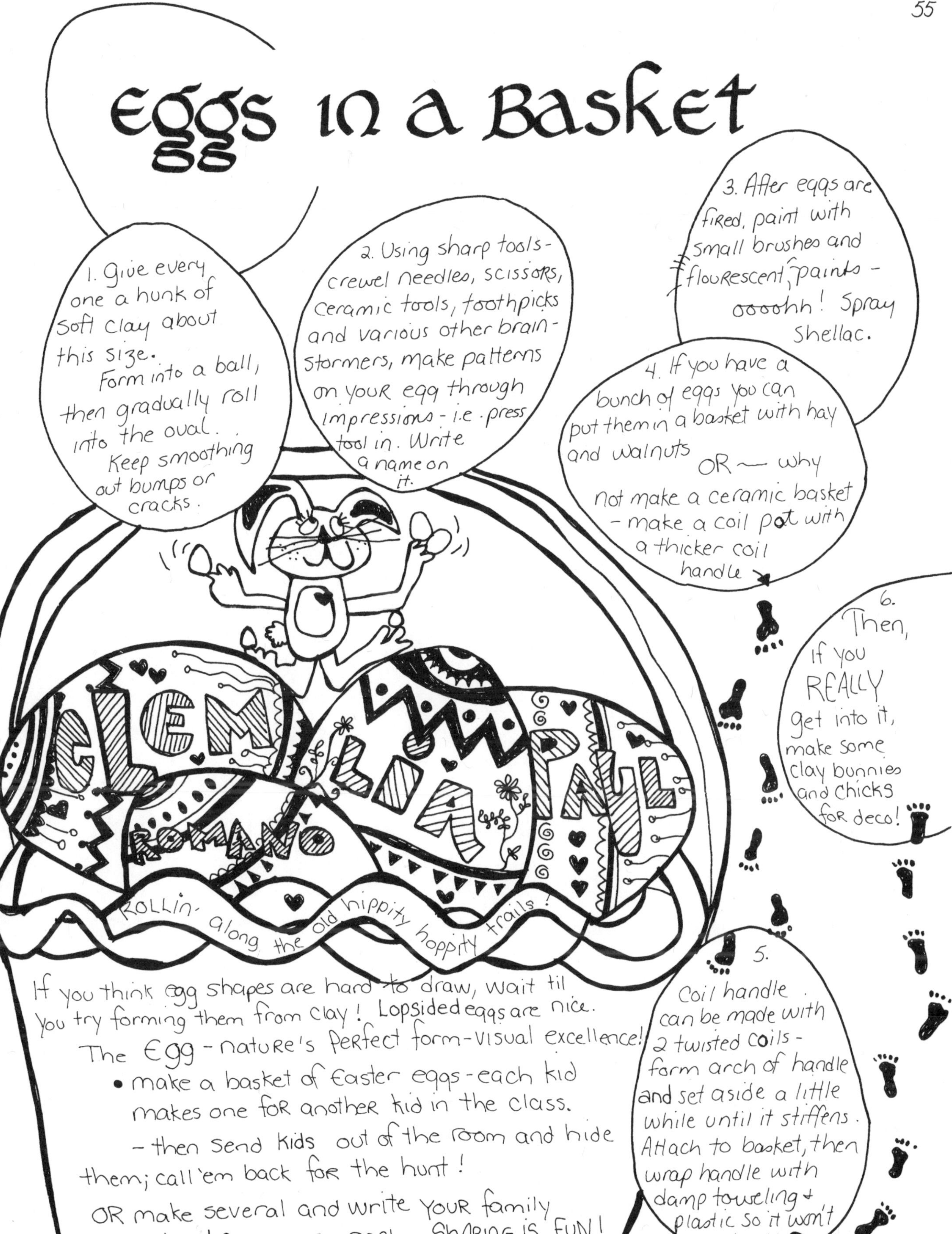
Eggs in a Basket
1. Give every one a hunk of soft clay about this size. Form into a ball, then gradually roll into the oval. Keep smoothing out bumps or cracks.
2. Using sharp tools - crewel needles, scissors, ceramic tools, toothpicks and various other brain-stormers, make patterns on your egg through impressions - i.e. press tool in. Write a name on it.
3. After eggs are fired, paint with small brushes and flourescent paints - oooohh! Spray Shellac.
4. If you have a bunch of eggs you can put them in a basket with hay and walnuts OR — why not make a ceramic basket - make a coil pot with a thicker coil handle
5. Coil handle can be made with 2 twisted coils - form arch of handle and set aside a little while until it stiffens. Attach to basket, then wrap handle with damp toweling + plastic so it won't crack off.
6. Then, if you REALLY get into it, make some clay bunnies and chicks for deco!
CLEM
LIA
PAUL
ROMANO
ROLLIN' along the old hippity hoppity trails!
If you think egg shapes are hard to draw, wait til you try forming them from clay! Lopsided eggs are nice.
The Egg - nature's perfect form - visual excellence!
• make a basket of Easter eggs - each kid makes one for another kid in the class.
- then send kids out of the room and hide them; call 'em back for the hunt!
OR make several and write your family members' names on each. SHARING IS FUN!

Papier - mâché

everyone enjoys the application of papier-mâché! strip by strip, layer by layer, the construction is all but monotonous and projects are only limited by the imagination.... which we all know
HAS NO LIMITS!!

★ ★ ★ ★ ★ ★ ★ ★ ★ wallpaper paste works great. ★ ★ ★

Let's Go!
you'll need:

1. Wheat Paste + water = mixture
   mix to rather thick consistency (goopey!) in a nice wide bowl - it thickens after setting 10 minutes.
2. Paper toweling cut into various size strips.
3. Odd paper, cardboard, wire, tape, newspaper for armature.

Basically, here's what you do:

1. Using newspaper, make basic shape - tape with masking tape.
2. Tape on major additions such as beak, eyes, major bumps, Adam's apples, trunks, fat stubby tails, horns, ears and so forth. (Use cardboard with substance, egg cartons, cereal boxes, etc.)
   - smaller details, such as teeth, antenna, eyeballs and tongues may be applied either in the process of mâché application or constructed with another media.

   1 2 3 4 - 4 layers
3. Dip toweling in mixture, removing excess; layer over work.
4. Paint when thoroughly dry - use poster (tempera) or acrylic.
5. Add decorative details, clothing, hair, props, finishing jobs.

thought kindlers

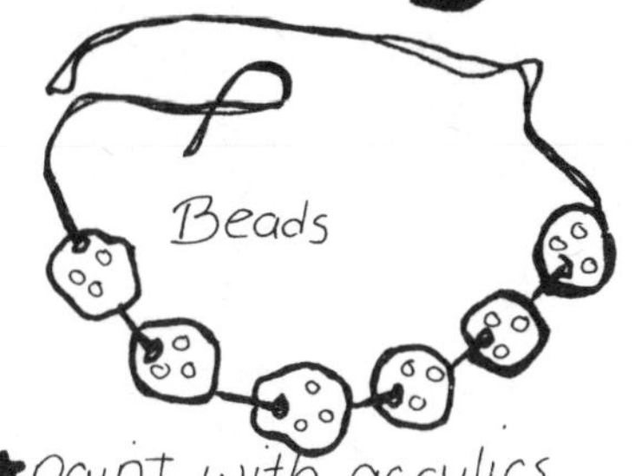

★paint with acrylics
★pierce holes with awl
★run rawhide through

PAUL

pins

★cut shape from corrugated cardboard; mâché
★paint with acrylics
★glue on pin back

★these can also be used as pendants

fine tipped markers may be used over acrylic paint for detailed things.

MAKE sure you smooth each layer!

fruit are easy and feel good to papier-mâché.

★ as an alternative to paint, torn tissue paper may be applied. Mix a solution of white glue and water and brush tissue over dried mâché forms.

Bowls come out irregularly shaped, but are still nice!

① real bowl is used as a form + PLUS + ② finish off edges

★Use 4-6 coats of toweling strips★

equals

bowls can be made by draping strips over a real bowl. When dry, remove form from real bowl and finish off edges near rim with more mâché strips. Coat with tissue; cut tissue shapes and superimpose; dry + shellac

☆ if tissue paper is used, overlap to achieve richer hues. You may also mix and blend with tissue ...experiment!

☆ after tissue paper has dried, brush over with shellac or polymer gloss for a shiny, protective coat.

ACROBATS

free moving

1. 2.

FLYING HIGH

★ Clowns ★ ballerinas ★ gorillas ★ monkeys

1. Make framework from wire - arms and legs may be made out of 4 pipe cleaners. Crumple up newspaper and tape within frame, giving bulk to body.
2. Coat body with papier-mâché strips, making certain to leave arm and leg joints free to swing about.
3. Costume ★ ★ ★ the fun part! Paint it on or, better yet, use pieces of silk, satin, fur or any exciting circus fabric to design a garb for your selected acrobat. Be sure to create a matching hat under a head of hair.
4. Slip hand loops through small 8" dowel + tie with twine.

Relief mâché

Relief - projection of figures or ornaments from the background. -Merriam-Webster

Interesting relief effects can be accomplished by saturating paper toweling strips in the wheat paste (mâché) mixture and laying shapes onto a background of corrugated cardboard. Cut a variety of strip sizes so that you can get large areas covered, then smaller details overlaying the large sections. Do your main background images first, then build up, getting more ornamental detail as you go. After the mâché dries, paint with temperas.

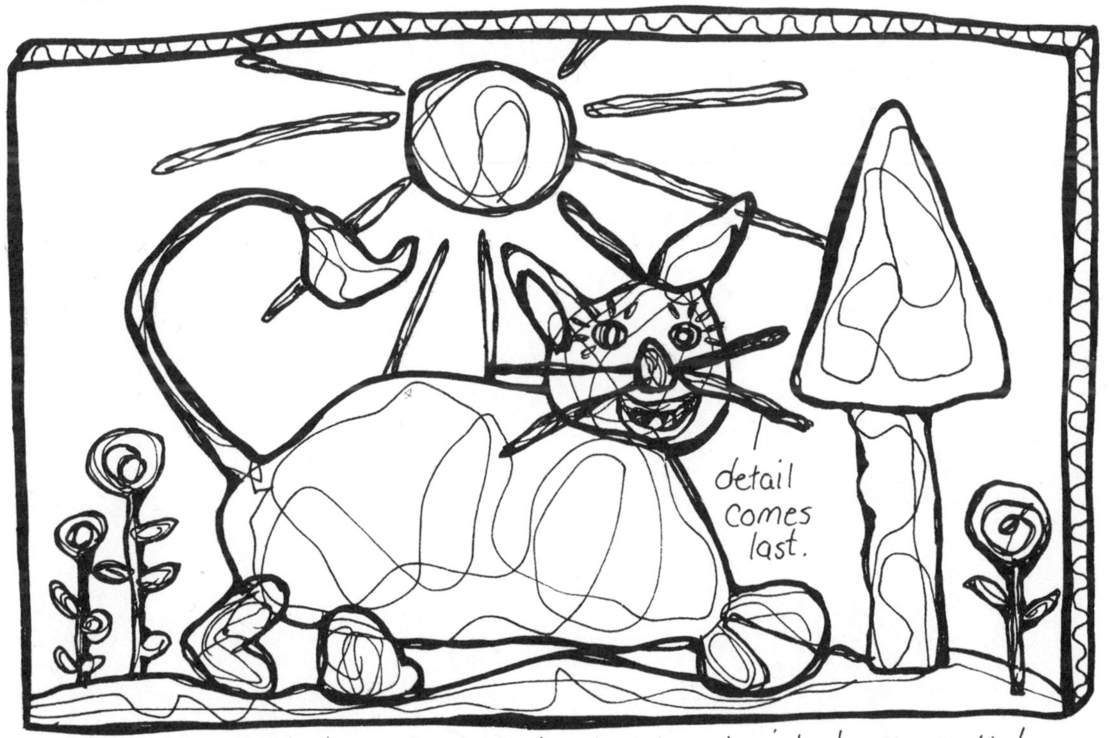

experiment with toweling manipulation - twist, ball, roll!

Ring toss

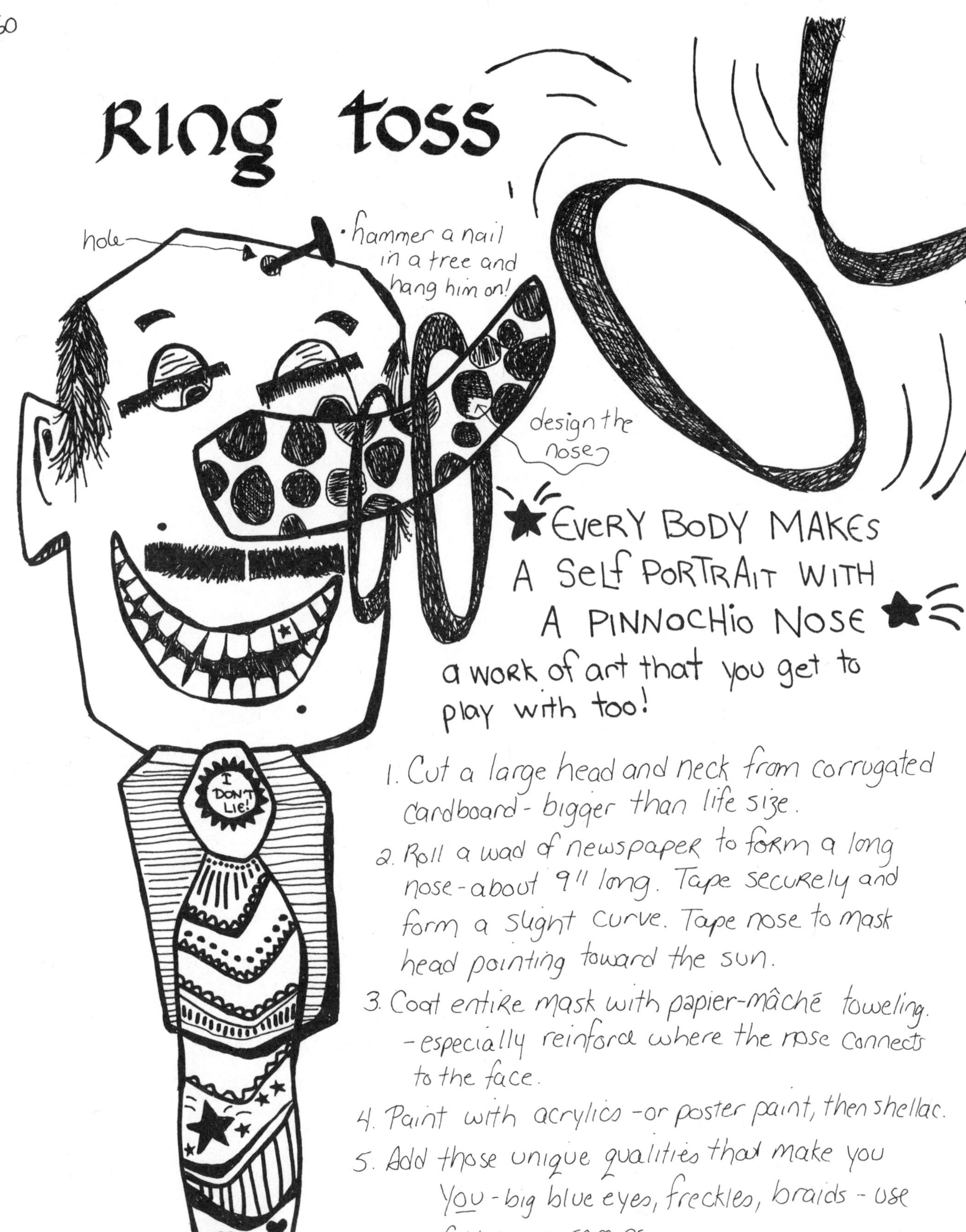

★ EVERY BODY MAKES A SELF PORTRAIT WITH A PINNOCHIO NOSE ★

a work of art that you get to play with too!

1. Cut a large head and neck from corrugated cardboard - bigger than life size.
2. Roll a wad of newspaper to form a long nose - about 9" long. Tape securely and form a slight curve. Tape nose to mask head pointing toward the sun.
3. Coat entire mask with papier-mâché toweling. - especially reinforce where the nose connects to the face.
4. Paint with acrylics - or poster paint, then shellac.
5. Add those unique qualities that make you <u>You</u> - big blue eyes, freckles, braids - use felt, yarn, scraps.
6. Make rings from cardboard - 1" by 14" - staple closed or * thick reed, tapped closed. Toss away!

Chick in an egg

Chick

Here A Chick • there a chick • everywhere a Chick!!

fun to make, delightful to view - hang 'em from the ceiling at different levels - hang them over a potted plant in a corner.

1. Using wads of newspaper, shape a simple chick - smaller than the size balloon you intend to use. Tape securely and coat with 3 layers of papier-mâché toweling strips - smoothly!
2. Inflate a sturdy oval balloon and drape colored string (heavy) or rug yarn (which is saturated with mâché paste) over balloon. - leave an area slightly more open so you can insert your chick.
3. Paint chick when dry; glue on felt beak, eyes and wings.
4. Add pipe cleaner feet.
5. When string dries, remove withered balloon.
6. Stick in chick
7. Hang them both!

thread a needle with thin yarn and tie to top of egg, leaving a small loop - insert another piece of yarn through loop for hanging.

①

②

③,④

felt

pipe cleaners

Hanger Heads

SELF-PORTRAITS

Choose an outstanding feature about yourself and emphasize it in these hanger heads! i.e.- big blue eyes, curly black hair, golden braids, freckles, a big smile!. Everyone can have one of those - pass yours to a friend and watch it grow ◡ !

1. Stretch a hanger to form a face.
2. Pad with newspaper - tape securely.
3. Coat with 2-3 layers of mâché strips.
4. Paint face.
5. Make a yarn hairstyle - use roving.

roll it

fray it

chopped it makes a crew cut!

braid it

MARDI GRAS MASKS

Noah's ark

can be made life size!!

A wanderful group project

5 or 6 people can work on the ark. the ark is made from corrugated cardboard boxes. Utility knives are helpful in cutting curves and portholes. If the curve is too difficult, an ark can be easily improvised by using a smaller box sitting inside a larger one, then adding a slant roof.

not as authentic but when it's surrounded with people and animals, it'll be just fine!

outside of ark can be padded with newspaper for softer look.
- when the ark is sturdily constructed, give it a layer of mâché, then paint it.

Each kid picks her favorite animal or family member to do. To construct animals and people, make body parts from newspaper - balled, rolled or crumpled and secured with masking tape. Really wrap tape to secure parts. Cover with mâché strips. paint. Use yarn, burlap and scraps for hair, features, and clothing. Show pictures of animals. Talk about people way back then.

there were seven people on the ark— Noah, and his family. What most people don't know is that the only animals that went in two by two were the scavengers -*OINK*- They were sent in to keep things clean inside. There were lots of every other kind of animal.

stocking-faced animals

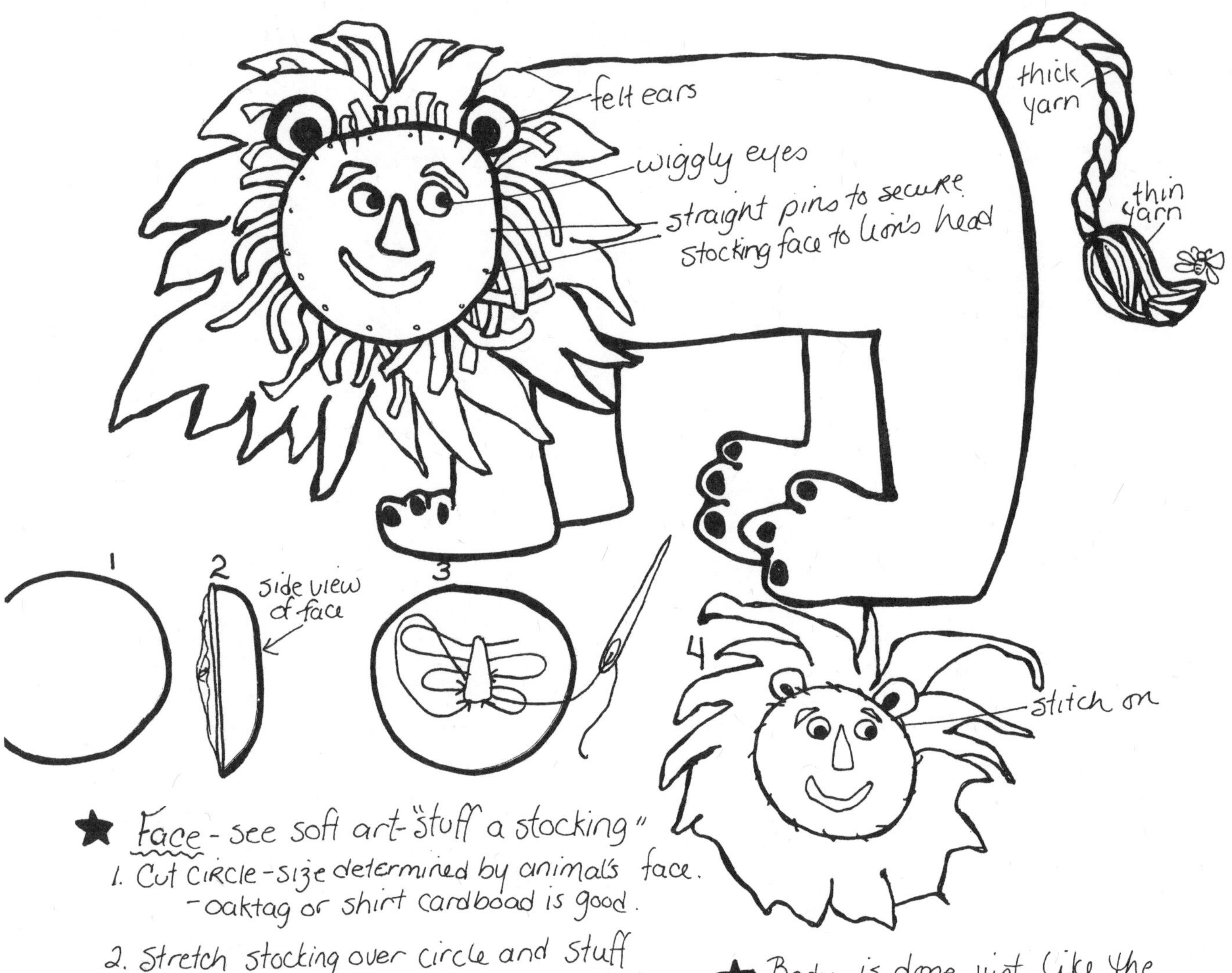

★ Face - see soft art "stuff a stocking"

1. Cut circle - size determined by animal's face.
   - oaktag or shirt cardboard is good.
2. Stretch stocking over circle and stuff with polyfiberfill. Stitch stocking to back.
3. Stitch features - movable "wiggly eyes" are fun on these.
4. Surround by hair (yarn) or mane (fur) (stitch edge of stocking to fur or yarn)
5. Using straight pins, push pin through head and into papier-mâché head.

★ Body is done just like the animals in Noah's ark - but make front part of head flat!

- felt stripes for zebras
- fake fur for lion's mane
- pipe cleaner whiskers
- roving hair, tails
- cotton bunny tails

Papier Mâché Balloons

Balloons balloons Balloons Balloons
are a kid's best friend!

A balloon base makes an excellent beginning to a myriad of creative activities. Inflate a heavy quality balloon and get going! give the balloon 4-6 coats of papier mâché. Make sure you smooth each strip you apply.

Cut opening - paint inside of egg as well as outside; stick a friend inside!

Paint the whole balloon - tie a ribbon on top!

Make an Easter Crèche or a peek-a-boo egg!
Use a utility knife to cut egg;
design egg and paint it; fill with hay.
throw in jelly beans. Make a papier mâché chickee or ~ an Easter bunny!

Felt

yarn

paint on designs
use felt, feathers, beads, cardboard for embellisment.

cut egg in half to make a mask!

giant helmet masks!
great for HALLOWeen!
★ pumpkin heads
★ goblins
★ ghosts
– simply cut head opening on bottom!

OVER MODELING CLAY

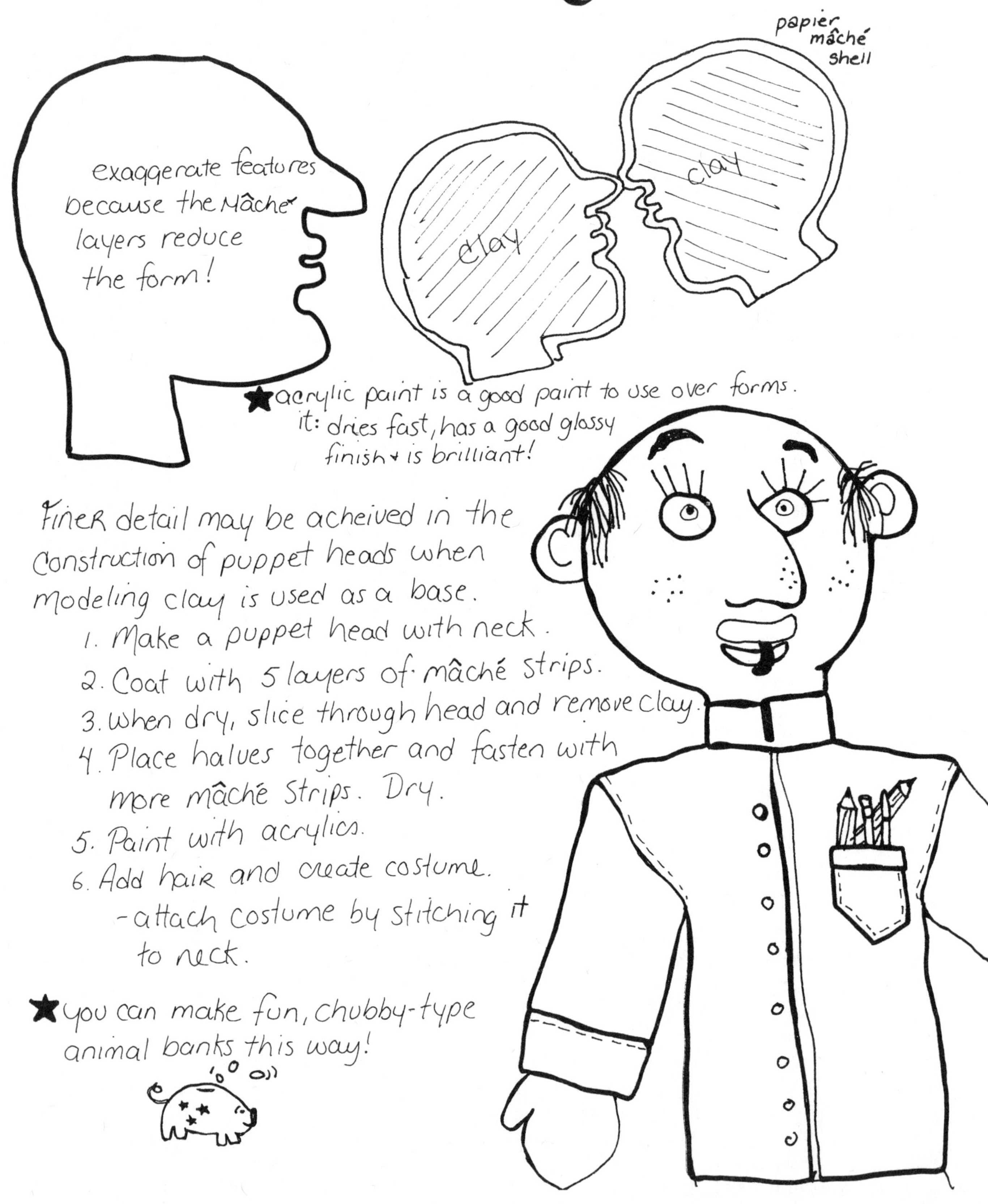

★ acrylic paint is a good paint to use over forms. it: dries fast, has a good glossy finish + is brilliant!

Finer detail may be acheived in the construction of puppet heads when modeling clay is used as a base.

1. Make a puppet head with neck.
2. Coat with 5 layers of mâché strips.
3. When dry, slice through head and remove clay.
4. Place halves together and fasten with more mâché strips. Dry.
5. Paint with acrylics.
6. Add hair and create costume.
   - attach costume by stitching it to neck.

★ you can make fun, chubby-type animal banks this way!

SWINGIN' KIDS

Kids are fun ♥
Swings are fun ♥
Make a kid on a
SWING*!!!!!!

Choose your favorite heroine* or, make yourself

1. Cut 6 sheets of newspaper to about a 9" by 12" size.
2. On the first sheet, draw your kid - keep her simple!
3. Spread papier-mâché mixture between each of the six layers of newspaper ~~ooooh~~!
4. Cut your kid out while she's wet and rest her in a sitting position on a shelf. You may have to brace her with a book so she won't sag while drying.
5. When dry, paint the kid, then dress her up with scrap fabrics and yarns.
6. Punch holes in hands and thread jute through - tie ends to a twig.
7. Tape bottom of her seat to twig so she sits securely.

salt Box hex
1.
2.
Slip in Some beans for noise
Cover part of dowel- top and bottom which extends from hex.
SHAKE THAT BABY!!
MILFORD CONN.
Save those egg cartons, oatmeal and Salt boxes – you've got a hex to perform!
1. Poke an 18" dowel through a cylindrical cardboard box. Tape. Cut eyes, nose, horns, etc. from egg carton - tape. Sneak in some beans!
2. Cover entire area with papier-mâché strips.
3. Paint with temperas.
4. Embellish with beans, bells, buttons, feathers and felt. You can wrap roving around stick, too.
5. While you're not busy hexing, stick them in a potted plant and place it at your bedroom door!

Detergent Folk

I always charge into the days of old lace and petticoats when I start tuning into detergent bottle folk. The natural form of the bottle is perfect for long robed people.

1. Crumple up newspaper and tape (with masking tape) into a ball - tape to top of bottle.
2. Roll newspaper into arm shapes and tape on.
3. Cover entire form with 3 coats of paper toweling coated with paper-mâché mixture
4. Dry and paint with temperas. Shellac for nice, shiny effect.
5. Gather bits of ric-rac, lace, yarn, felt and beads and authenticate your character.

You can: make dolls of the world, ballroom dancers, brides, Colonial folk, peasants or princesses.

- make little props for them to hold or wear - capes, umbrellas, etc.

MOBILES

~~~ a construction or sculpture with parts that can be set in motion by air currents.
~Merriam-Webster

Mobiles are a wind trip! They dance and twirl and become quasi-alive as the components take on animation with the slightest shift in the air. They've been around for centuries - we've all delighted in the old Chinese glass windbells — aahh! What form, what balance, how delicately musical these works of art!

★ Let's start out easily with coat hangers and cardboard.

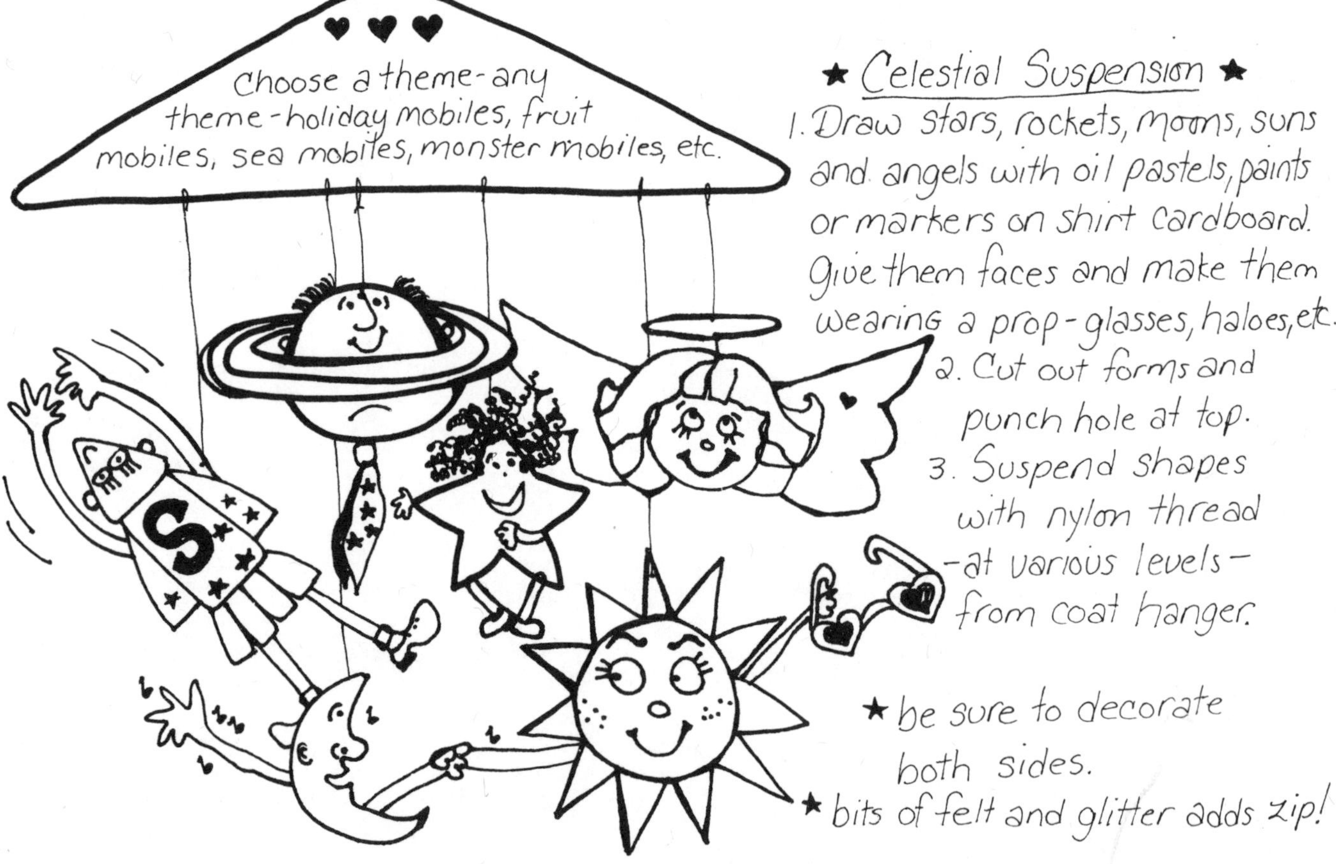

★ Celestial Suspension ★

1. Draw stars, rockets, moons, suns and angels with oil pastels, paints or markers on shirt cardboard. Give them faces and make them wearing a prop - glasses, haloes, etc.
2. Cut out forms and punch hole at top.
3. Suspend shapes with nylon thread - at various levels - from coat hanger.

★ be sure to decorate both sides.

★ bits of felt and glitter adds zip!
~~~

Watercolor Resist Mobile

1. Using oil pastels, decorate both sides of a paper plate-press firmly.
2. Brush over entire area with watercolor paints - blend colors that mix well together - yellows, greens, blues. Dry, then paint the other side.
3. Slit to center of plate, fold one section over and staple, forming a "coolie" hat.
4. Make animals with construction paper and oil pastels. glue on yarn hair.
5. Punch holes in animals and in carousel and suspend with bright yarn.

BIRD MOBILE

★ Wonderful spring lobby exhibits are a terrific group endeavor!

1. Make simple birds from construction paper, drawing body on the fold; wings are made on another piece of folded paper and may be cut out as one piece and laid over body, or cut separately and glued to sides.
2. Cut construction paper legs or.... poke in pipe cleaner legs.
3. Decorate with oil pastels, real feather tails and felt or seed eyes.
4. Tie birds to tree branch with nylon thread.
5. Tree branch may be stuck into large potted plant - with plant still in it!

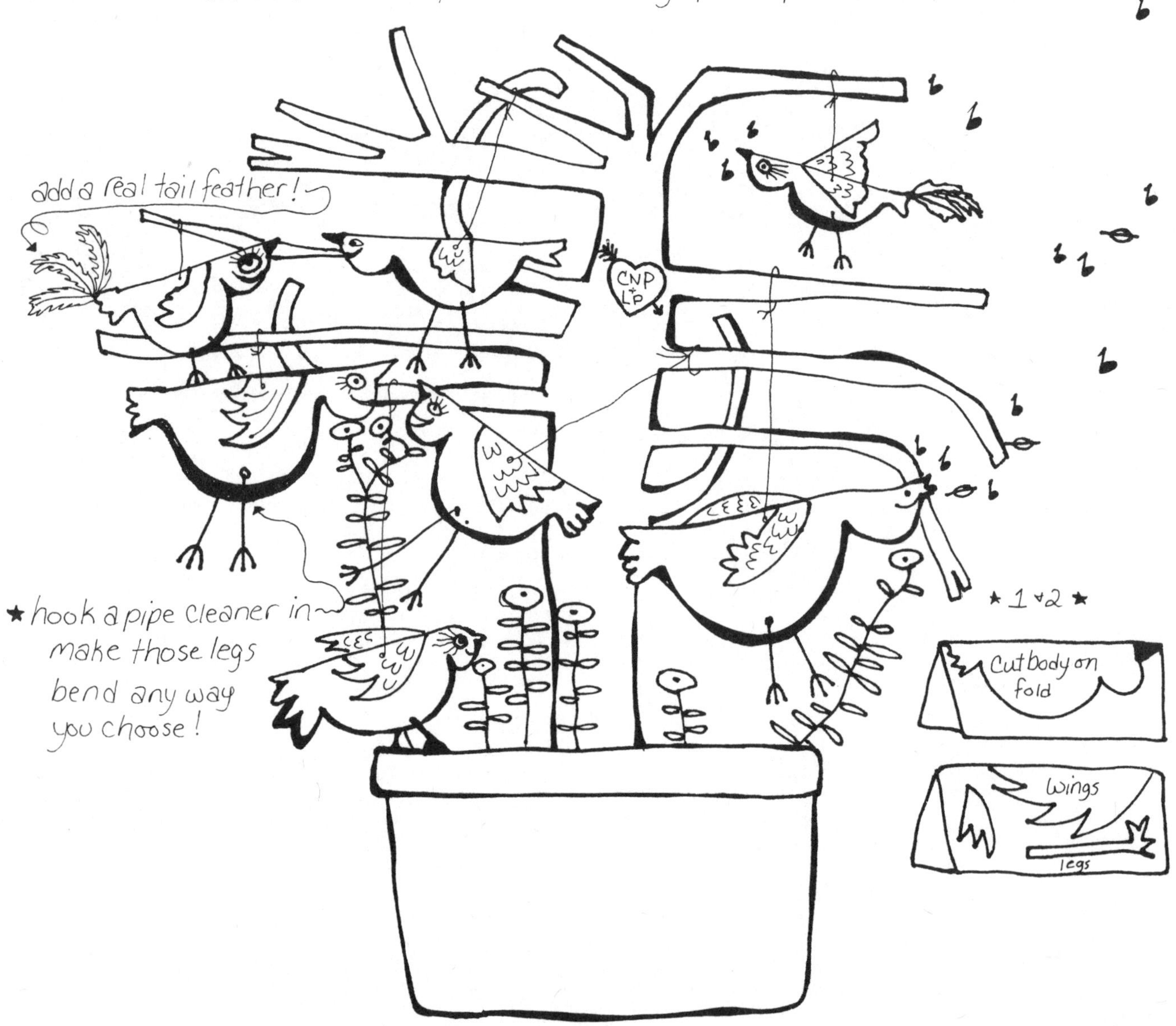

FISH MOBILE

Let's talk about BIG fish - how big was that whale that swallowed Jonah? Let's take a trip into the jaws of this meanie! What's cookin' in there?

1. Cut a very large fish from cardboard; cut a hole in its body.
2. Cut several smaller fish of all variety.
3. Decorate and color all fish - both sides, now - with markers.
4. Punch holes as indicated and tie with fishing line.

* small ones should be able to move freely without touching each other *

tin can bells

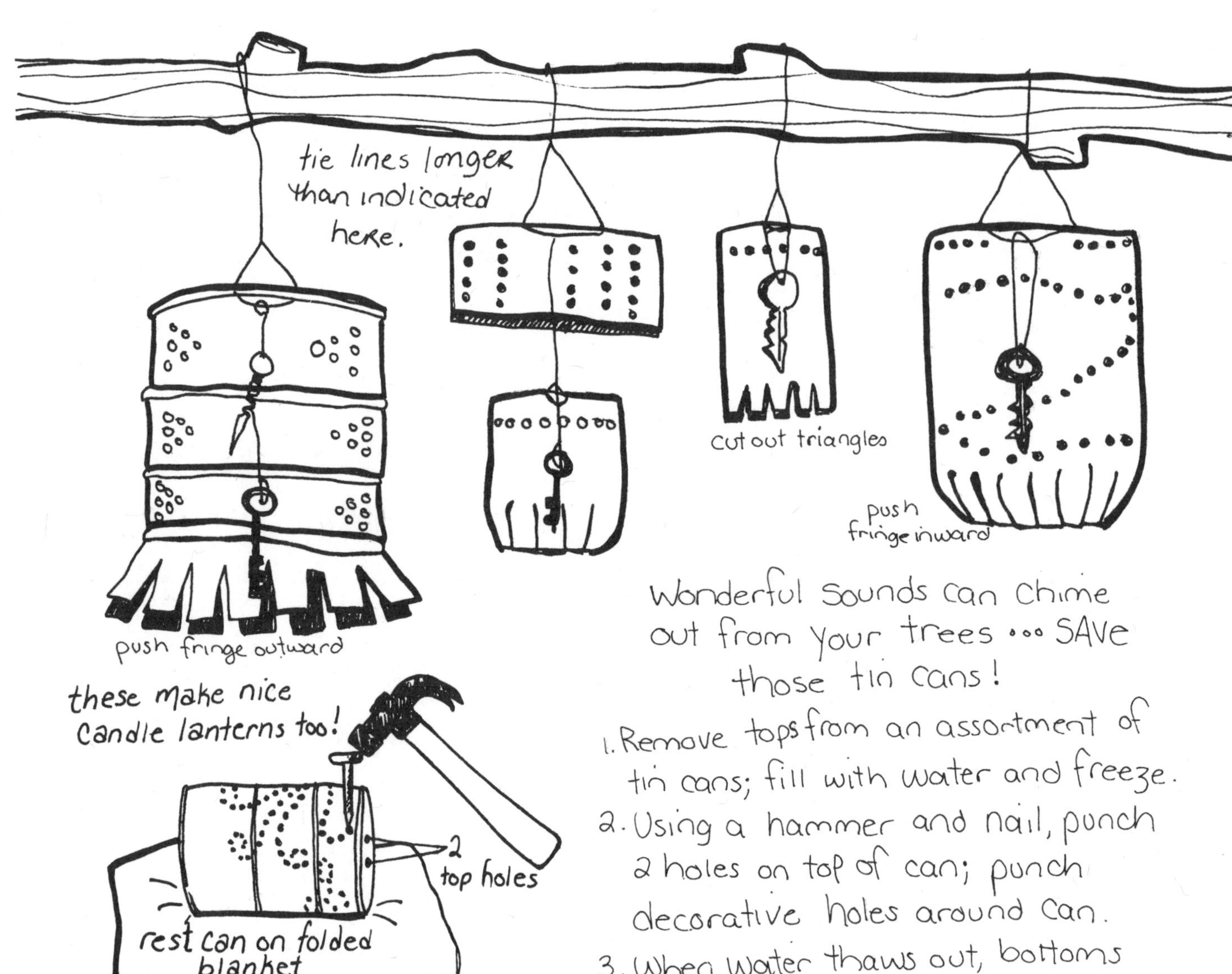

Wonderful sounds can chime out from your trees ... SAVE those tin cans!

1. Remove tops from an assortment of tin cans; fill with water and freeze.
2. Using a hammer and nail, punch 2 holes on top of can; punch decorative holes around can.
3. When water thaws out, bottoms of cans may be treated with slits and bent inward or outward.
   • Use a metel cutter for this and be careful of sharp edges!
4. With fishing line, tie a loop through old keys or other metal objects. Next, string fishing line through one top hole in can, through loop with key on it, then back up can through second hole.
5. Tie knot, then draw line up to tree branch—hang bells at different levels. Key should hit sides of can freely.

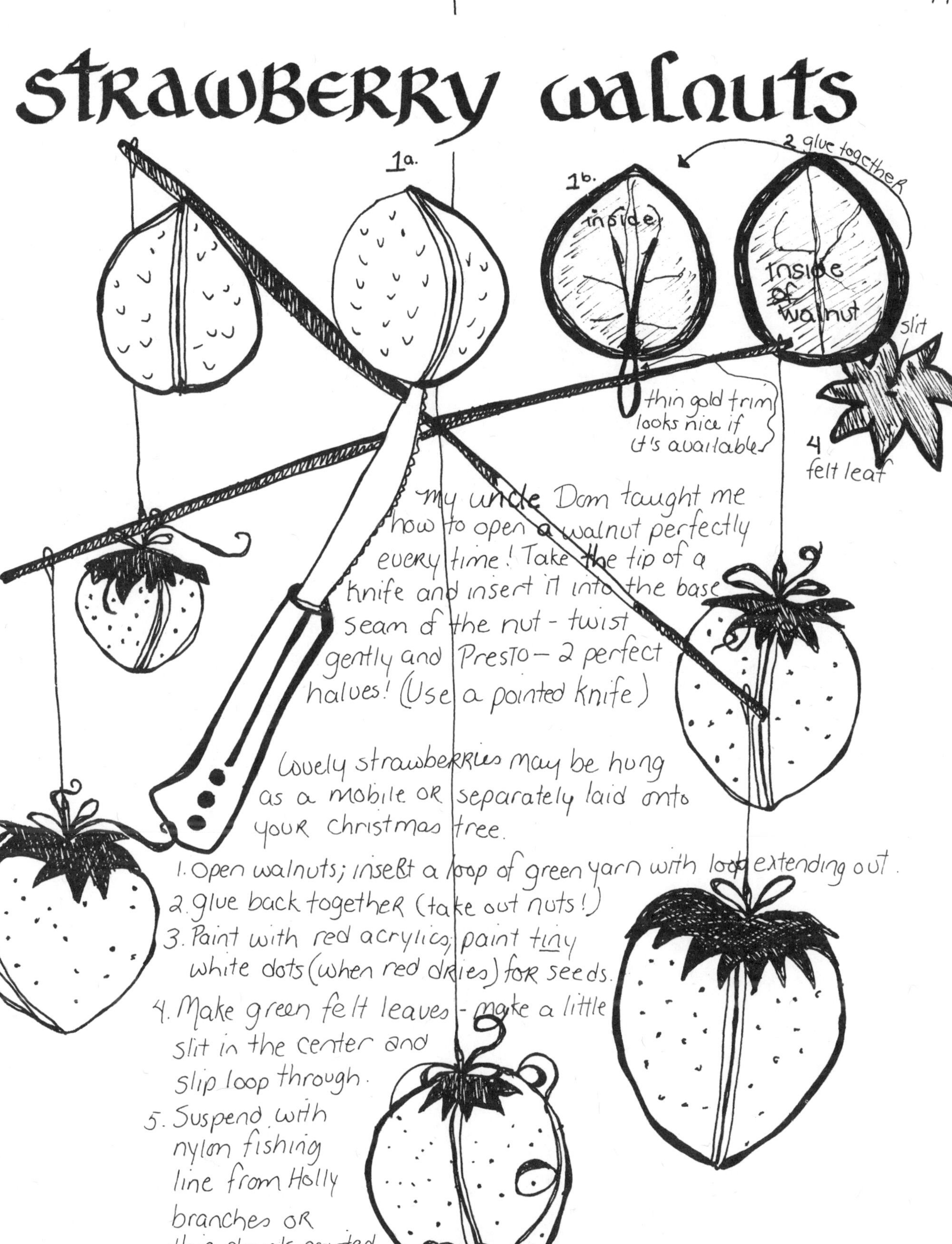
Strawberry walnuts
1a.
1b.
inside
2 glue together
Inside of walnut
slit
thin gold trim looks nice if it's available
4 felt leaf
my uncle Dom taught me how to open a walnut perfectly every time! Take the tip of a knife and insert it into the base seam of the nut - twist gently and Presto — 2 perfect halves! (Use a pointed knife)
Lovely strawberries may be hung as a mobile or separately laid onto your christmas tree.
1. Open walnuts; insert a loop of green yarn with loop extending out.
2. glue back together (take out nuts!)
3. Paint with red acrylics; paint tiny white dots (when red dries) for seeds.
4. Make green felt leaves - make a little slit in the center and slip loop through.
5. Suspend with nylon fishing line from Holly branches or thin dowels painted green.

VALENTINE BIRDS

LOVEBIRDS

1. Glue a doily onto a 9" red oaktag circle.
2. Slit circle from edge to center and staple, forming a coolie hat.
3. Make bird body by cutting ½ a heart on the fold of a rectangle of red construction paper.
4. Wings are ½ heart cut on open edge.
5. Make paper beaks and legs; glue to inside of heart.
6. Glue heart closed, glue on wings.
7. Decorate bird with bits of doily and markers.
8. Punch hole in birds and around coolie frame; suspend with thread.

SPIRALS

fig. A cut

MORE Indian INSPIRATION

Make a simply delightful bird mobile with a simple oaktag circle 9-12" diameter. Cut along the dotted lines as shown above (fig. A)

Make birds from an assortment of different colors of construction paper.

Design and color both sides with oil pastels.

- Cut them out.
- Punch appropriate holes in spiral and in birds.

Suspend with embroidery thread.

these delightful bird designs are taken from ceramics of Southwestern American Indians 19th CENTURY

these animal figures are taken from Mimbres black and white pottery — they were painted inside of ceramic bowls. 1000 A.D.

DISPOSABLE DELIGHTS

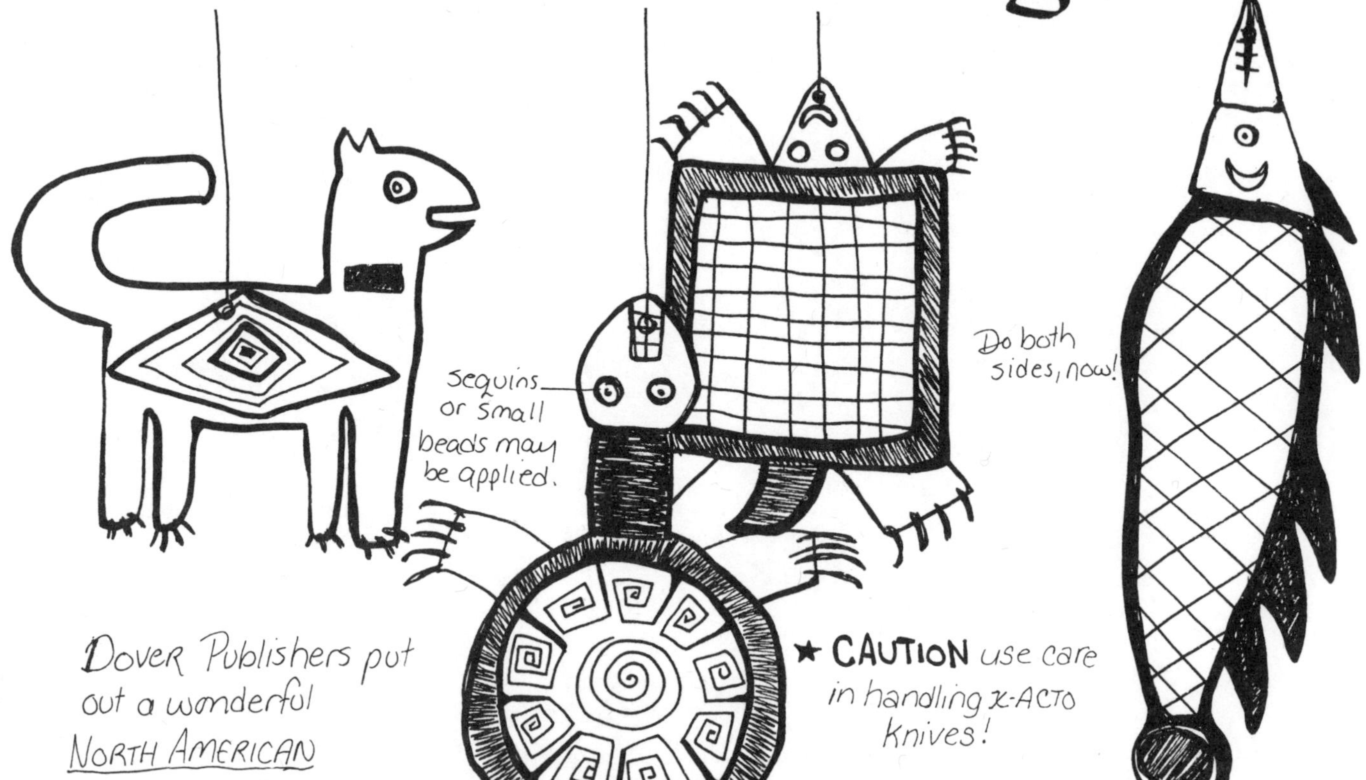

★ **CAUTION** use care in handling X-ACTO knives!

Dover Publishers put out a wonderful NORTH AMERICAN Indian Design coloring book (rendered by Paul E. Kennedy). This book contains lots of designs illustrating the fullness of North American Indian art, from the Eskimos through the great Plains to the great Lakes. The images used by the Indians are very well suited in embellishing our own work and allowing inspirational growth to flourish through our Souls!

1. Using an X-ACTO knife, carefully cut simple mobile shapes - do not make intricate lines!
2. Apply a shield of tooled aluminum over styrofoam with glue. (Tooling is making a designed impression on the aluminum with a sharp object (pencil) Tool over a padding of paper toweling.

These mobiles combine those disposable aluminum and styrofoam meat and vegetable trays - Save them!

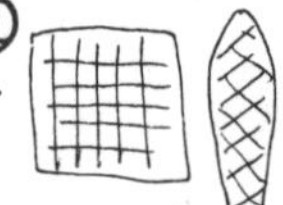

3. Cut smaller pieces of aluminum to apply delicate details - claws, collars, teeth, etc.
   - make sure metal is free of dirt or oil, or it won't stick to styrofoam
4. Suspend from branch with nylon thread.

DOUGH ORNAMENTS

BAKED ORNAMENTS

can be hung from dried branches, from cup hooks in the ceiling, on Christmas trees or over your kitchen sink.

RECIPE: 4 C. flour
1 C. salt
1½ C. water

} mix to workable consistency - add more water if it's too stiff

1. Shape ornaments over wax paper.
2. Apply decorative embellishments through coils, small balls and impressions made with shape tools.
3. Bend a piece of wire into a hook and slip into top of ornament.
4. Bake for one hour at 300° F.
5. Paint when cool with enamels, acrylics or temperas. (Tempera paint should be shellacked over for preservation.)

• food coloring may be mixed right in the dough for penetrated color.

Crayon Laminations

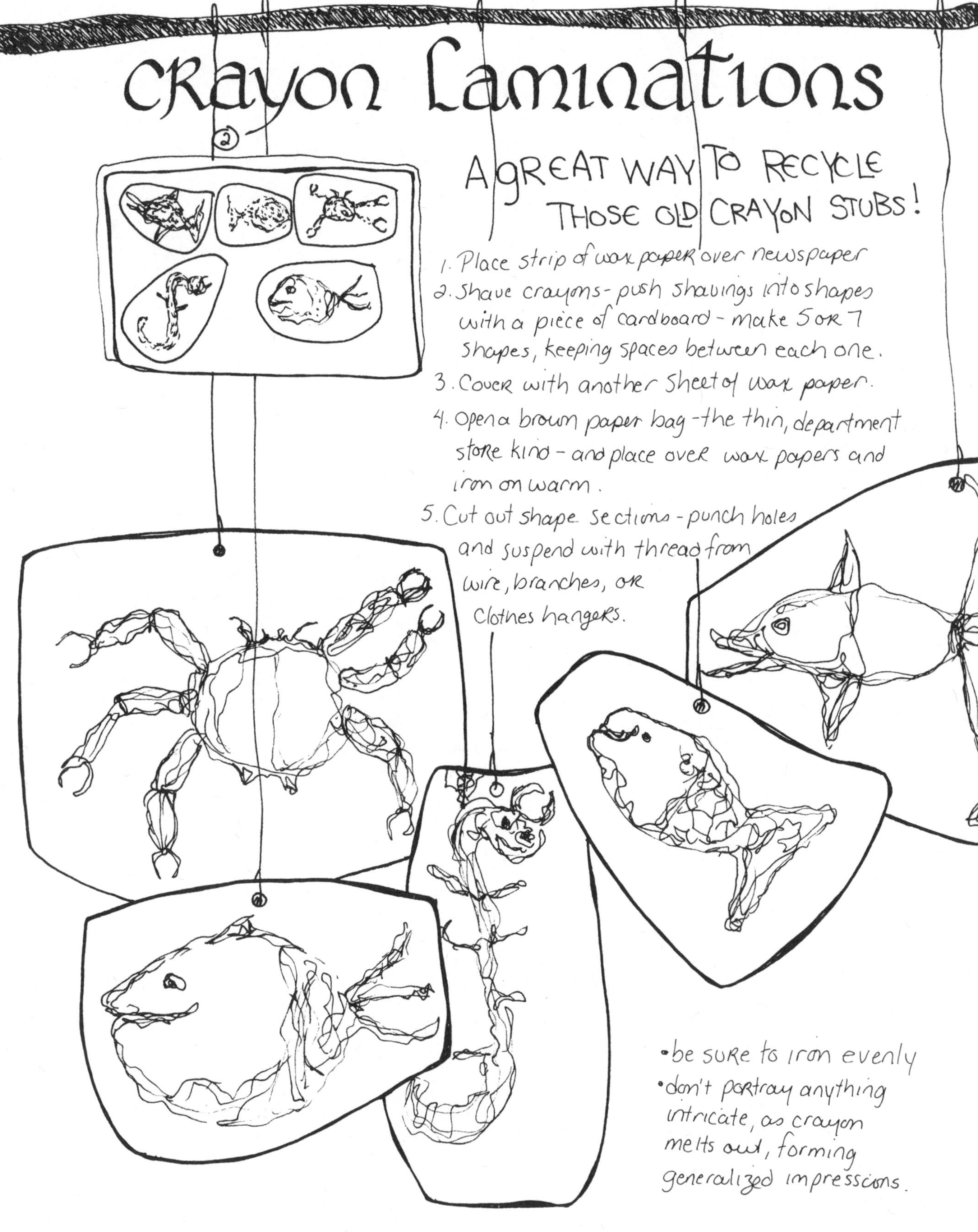

A GREAT WAY TO RECYCLE THOSE OLD CRAYON STUBS!

1. Place strip of wax paper over newspaper
2. Shave crayons - push shavings into shapes with a piece of cardboard - make 5 or 7 shapes, keeping spaces between each one.
3. Cover with another sheet of wax paper.
4. Open a brown paper bag - the thin, department store kind - and place over wax papers and iron on warm.
5. Cut out shape sections - punch holes and suspend with thread from wire, branches, or clothes hangers.

- be sure to iron evenly
- don't portray anything intricate, as crayon melts out, forming generalized impresscions.

COOKIE CUTTER SUSPENSIONS

Get out those tin cookie cutters - they're perfect for cutting shapes out of a thin slab of clay. Or, follow the recipe for baked dough ornaments. Clay or baked dough can be painted with enamels or acrylics.

Clay cut shapes make delightful sounds.

Hang with fishing line from driftwood.

Natural Delights

Natural Design far surpasses our own comprehension. Take a walk through the woods and pick up a mushroom or a pine cone - the designs are beautiful. Stroll to the beach and watch a sunrise. Collect shells. Zoom in on the delicate lines and subtle colors created on a crab shell. Study the colors painted on stones. Feel some driftwood. Pick up some favorites - especially natural objects with holes already there. String them from fishing line to a pine cone branch or driftwood.

Human Mobiles

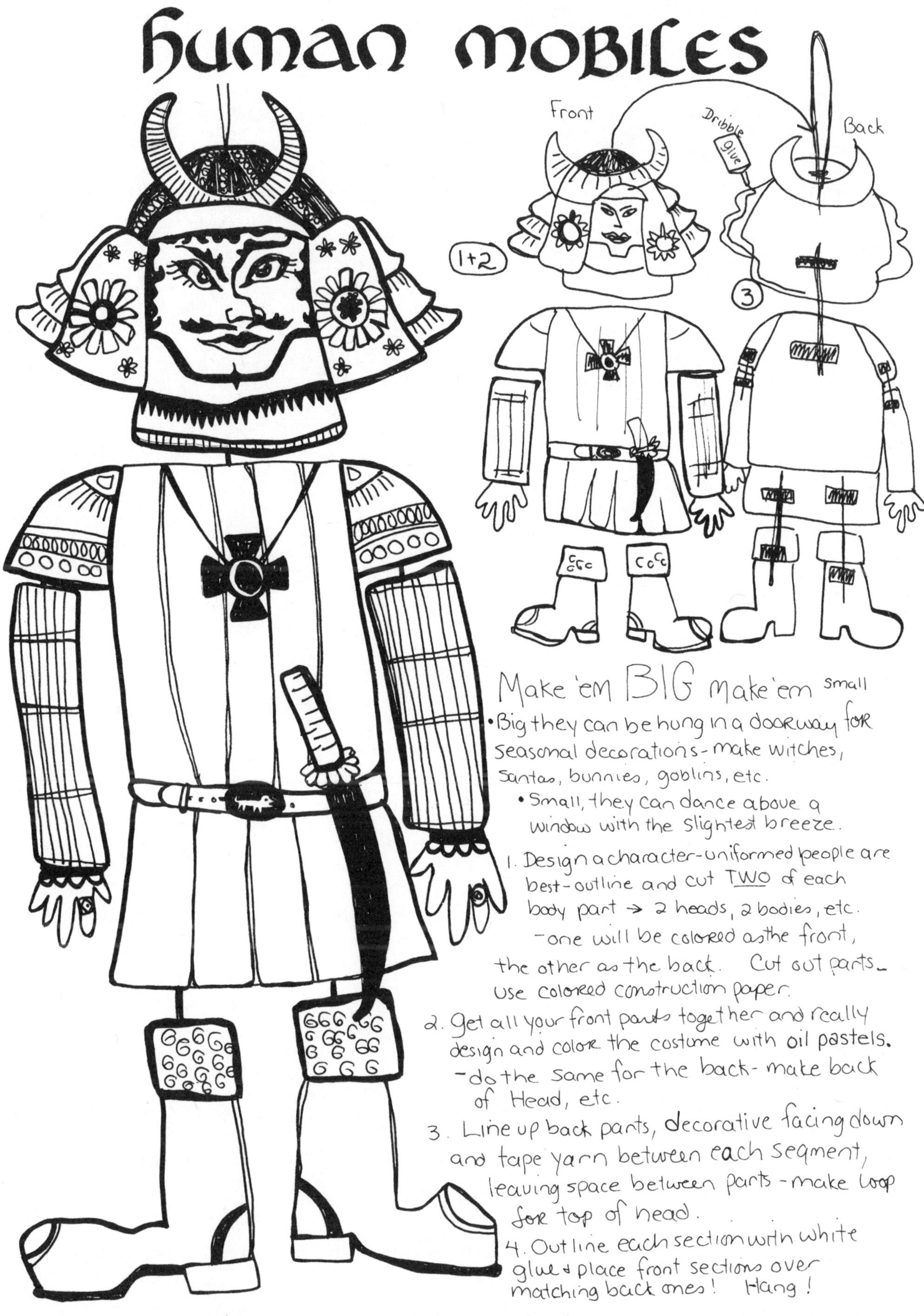

Make 'em BIG make 'em small

- Big they can be hung in a doorway for seasonal decorations - make witches, Santas, bunnies, goblins, etc.
  - Small, they can dance above a window with the slightest breeze.

1. Design a character - uniformed people are best - outline and cut TWO of each body part → 2 heads, 2 bodies, etc.
   - one will be colored as the front, the other as the back. Cut out parts - use colored construction paper.
2. Get all your front parts together and really design and color the costume with oil pastels.
   - do the same for the back - make back of Head, etc.
3. Line up back parts, decorative facing down and tape yarn between each segment, leaving space between parts - make loop for top of head.
4. Outline each section with white glue & place front sections over matching back ones! Hang!

★ Cardboard should be of substantial thickness or it will warp from the glue.

★ do both sides of animals with yarn.

TRADITIONAL AFRICAN IMAGES are wonderful decorative motifs for pottery, tooling, mâché sculpture, masks and suspended forms. These animal images are taken from various African tribal designs. Their simplistic beauty lends themselves to a myriad of inspirational creative leads.

YARN ANIMAL Mobiles

1. Cut a simple animal shape from cardboard - corrugated works well, although it's a little difficult to cut.

2. Pencil in designs - try not to get lots of choppy or angular lines, as yarn isn't best suited toward these types.

3. Using white glue, outline penciled areas, then lay yarn over glue.

4. Tiny beads make wonderful eyes.

5. Suspend from a branch or a 2" by 18" strip of oaktag stapled to form a ring.

TISSUE AND REED

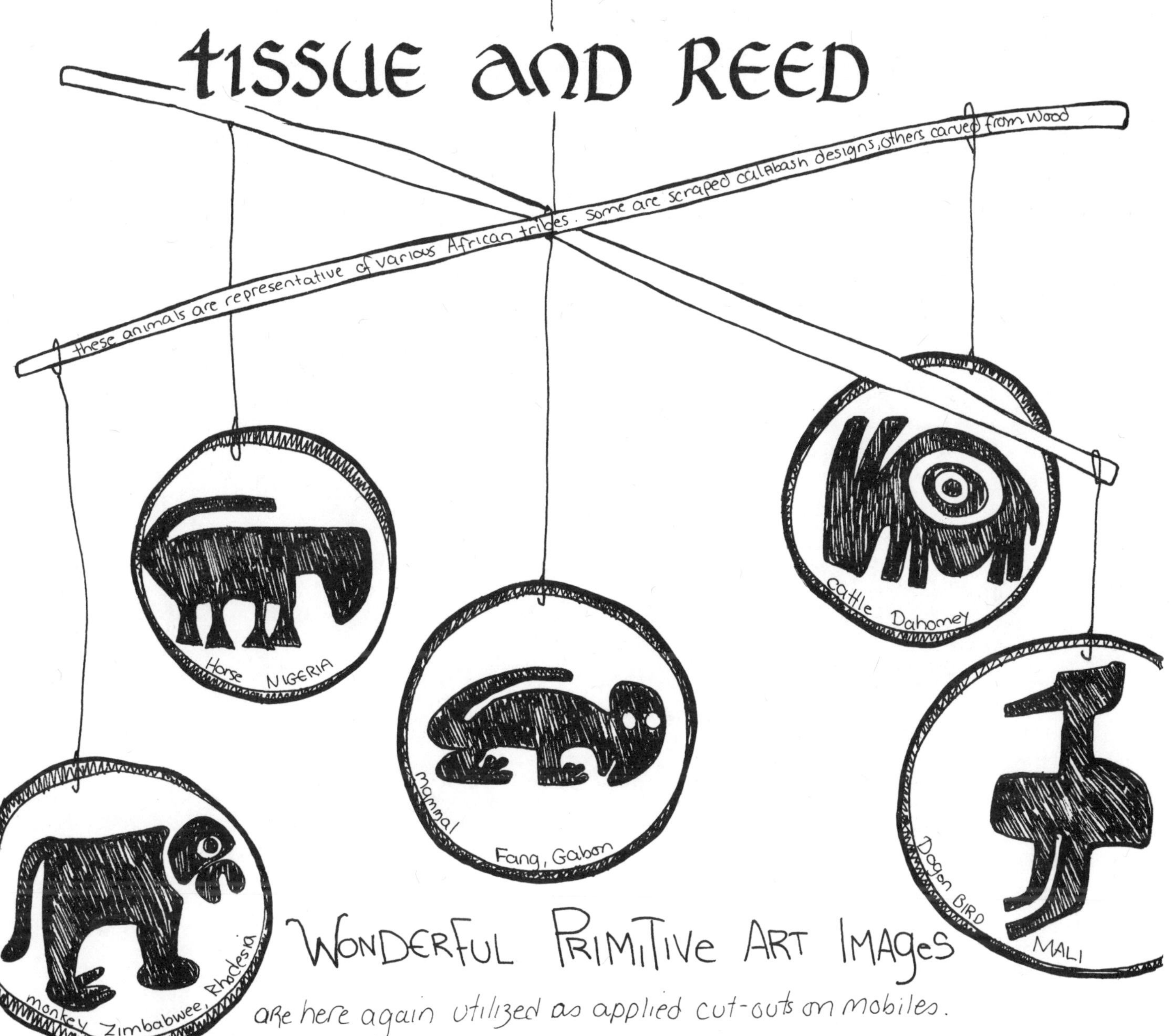

WONDERFUL PRIMITIVE ART IMAGES are here again utilized as applied cut-outs on mobiles.

1. Make a reed ring with a 4-5" diameter - tape with masking tape.
2. Coat rim with white glue, then lay on colored tissue paper - trim to circle.
3. Using thinner thickness black construction paper make related objects that will fit within circle. (Trees, flowers, birds, fish, insects, etc.)
4. Using rubber cement, coat back of images and apply to tissued ring. (If you are a precisionist, you can make doubles of each form and glue one to the front and one to the back - in the same spot on each side)
5. Suspend with your nylon thread from dowels or reed.

planet panoramas

A Mobile in a Box

Shoebox panoramas are great for school projects- science-social-studies fairs, acquarium exhibits or insects in flight. They're portable and can be made with stuff found around the house. Take a shoebox and paint it- inside and out- make interior relate to theme— Starry night in this case. Make planets, suns, rockets, moons from construction paper-make 2 of each shape and glue string between shapes, then glue together. Tape string to top of box. (Small styrofoam balls make nice planets) Make sure you decorate both sides of each shape.

MONSTERMOBILE

Claw is made by inserting a firm wire about 12 inches in length within felt arm-claws.

Two lengths of felt, 12-13 inches long are cut to form arm-claws. Claws are over-cast stitched together.

GRRRREAT!!

hangamonster, why don't ya!?*

this monstermobile is an Eskimo seal design, enveloped by a claw. Any animal works well, the meaner, the better.

1. Cut 2 animal shapes from felt.
2. Stitch around animal, leaving opening for stuffing.
3. Stuff with polyfiberfill and close.
4. Surround with claw wire.
5. Suspend forms within each-other using thread.
6. Embellish with contrasting felt.

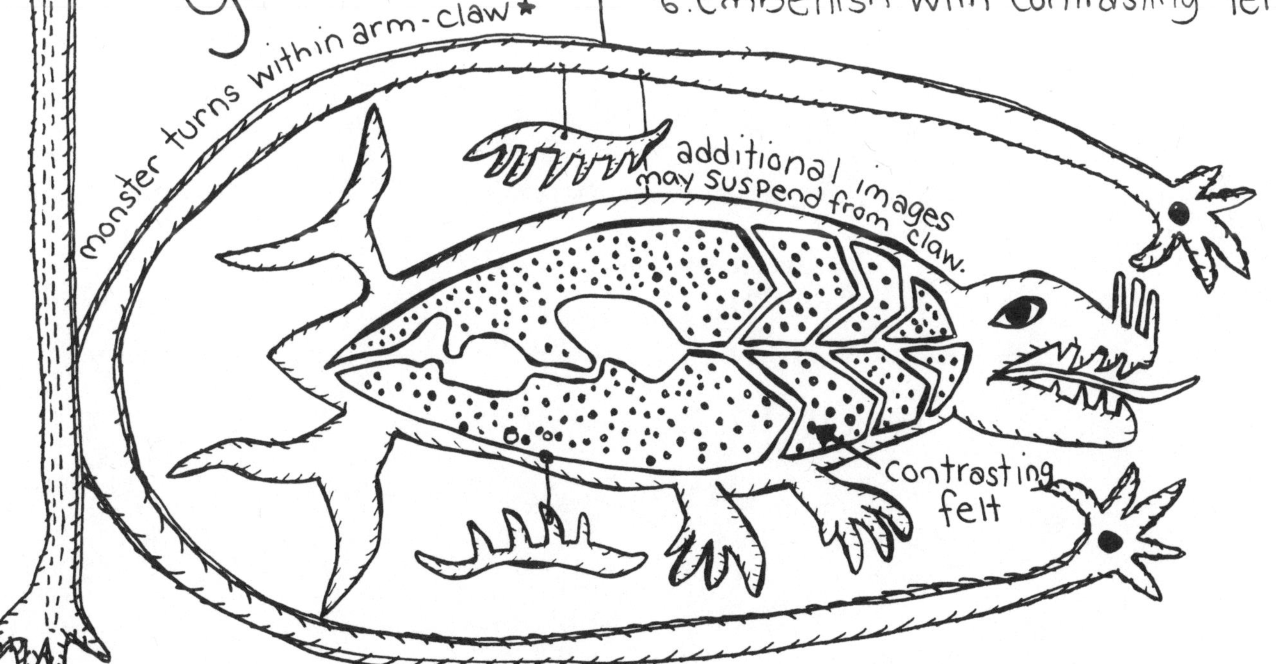

CARTOON MOBILES

Make cartoon characters with coat hangers, pipe cleaners, tin foil and tin or aluminum pie plates. Here's how: ① Stretch a coat hanger into a face.

② Cut features from a pie plate - poke holes through features and tie to wire or suspend from another wire - or feature. Or ➡ wrap feature around wire to make ears and beards.

tin plate eyelids

balled up tin foil eyeballs

If you place tin (aluminum) feature over a newspaper padding and draw with a blunt pencil, you'll get a nice embossed or tooled effect. Try it!

wrap beard around wire

ANIMOBILES

Animals from our Indian friends serve as wonderful animated suspensions. These animals derive from the Mimbres people, a Southwestern U.S. Indian tribe.

Cut forms from white shirt cardboard. Use fine-tipped permanent markers to outline inner markings. Embellish with bits of felt, tin foil, natural fibers and toothpicks.

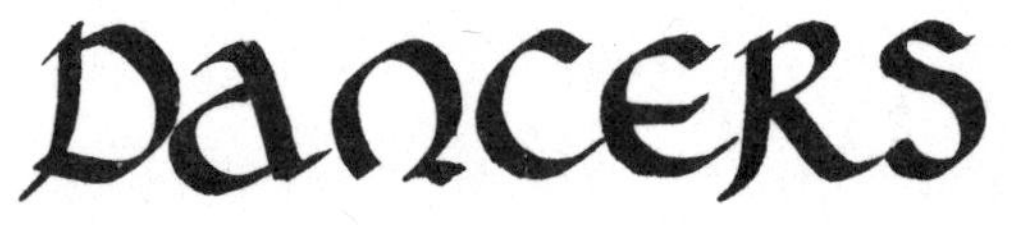

Dancers

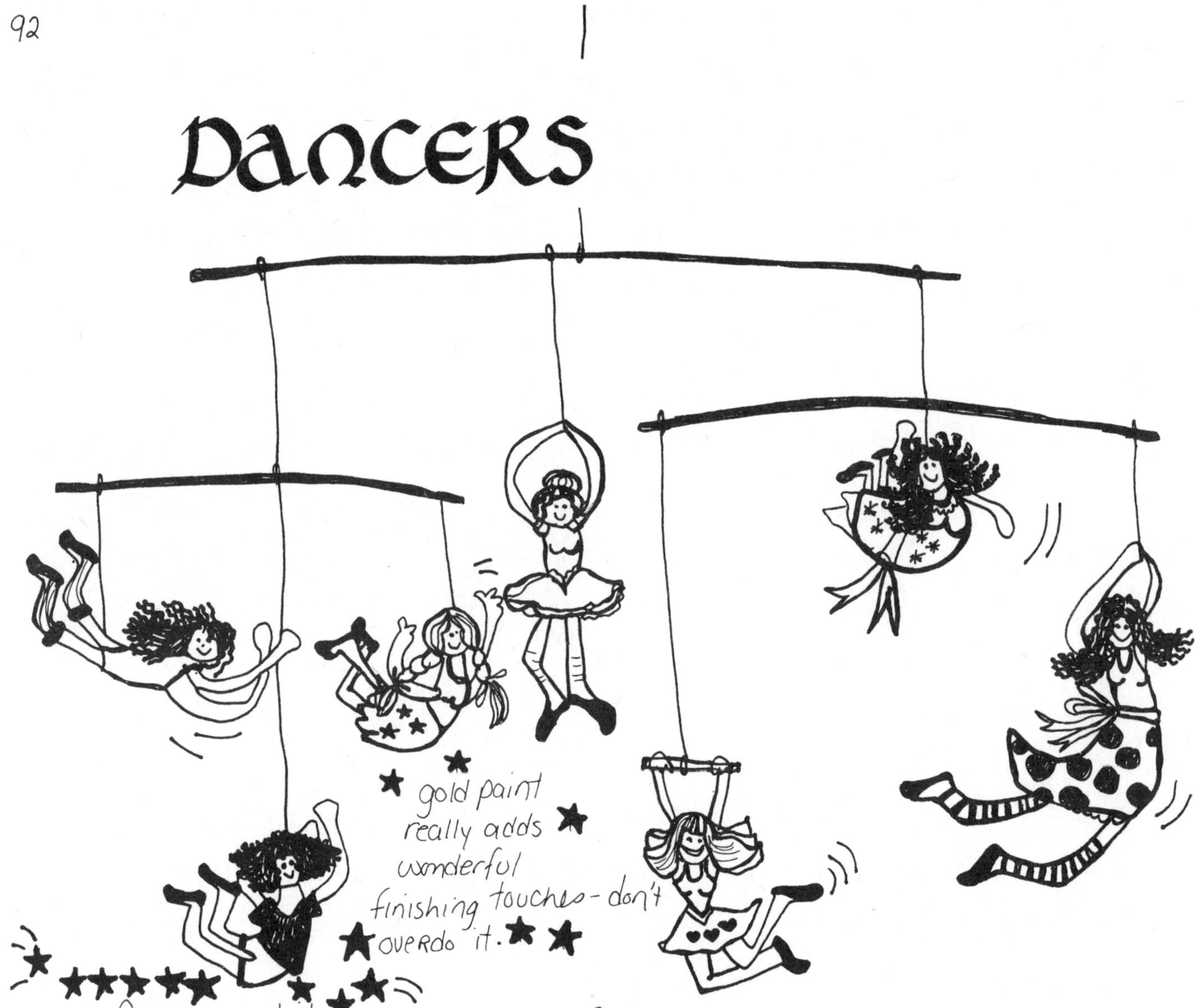
gold paint
really adds
wonderful
finishing touches - don't
overdo it.

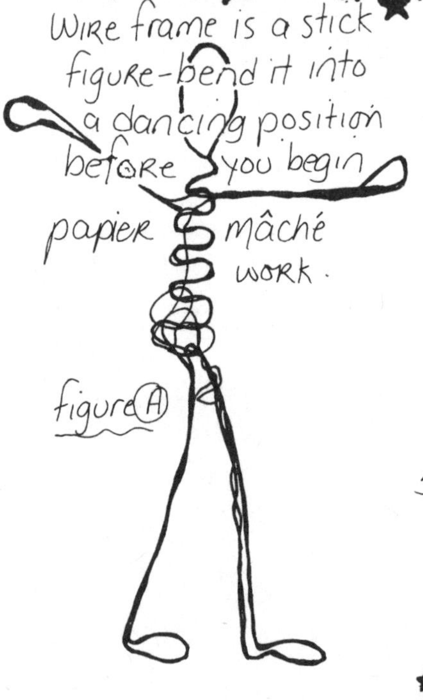
Wire frame is a stick
figure - bend it into
a dancing position
before you begin
papier mâché
work.
figure Ⓐ

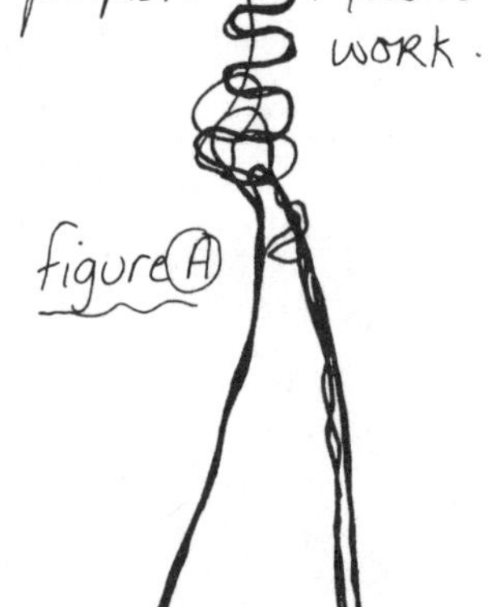

1. Make wire frames and cover with papier-mâché — see section on papier-mâché. Clothes can be formed from the toweling dipped in the mixture, then wrapped to create skirts and hair right on the figure.
2. Paint with acrylics.
4. Thread a needle with fishing line and poke through body at a point of balance.
5. Tie figures to lengths of wire; suspend.

★ bodies can be made with heavy pipe cleaners if they are no larger than figure Ⓐ.

★ they're nicer about 6" tall, but you'll need a heavier gauge, pliable type wire.

stuffed tissue stabile

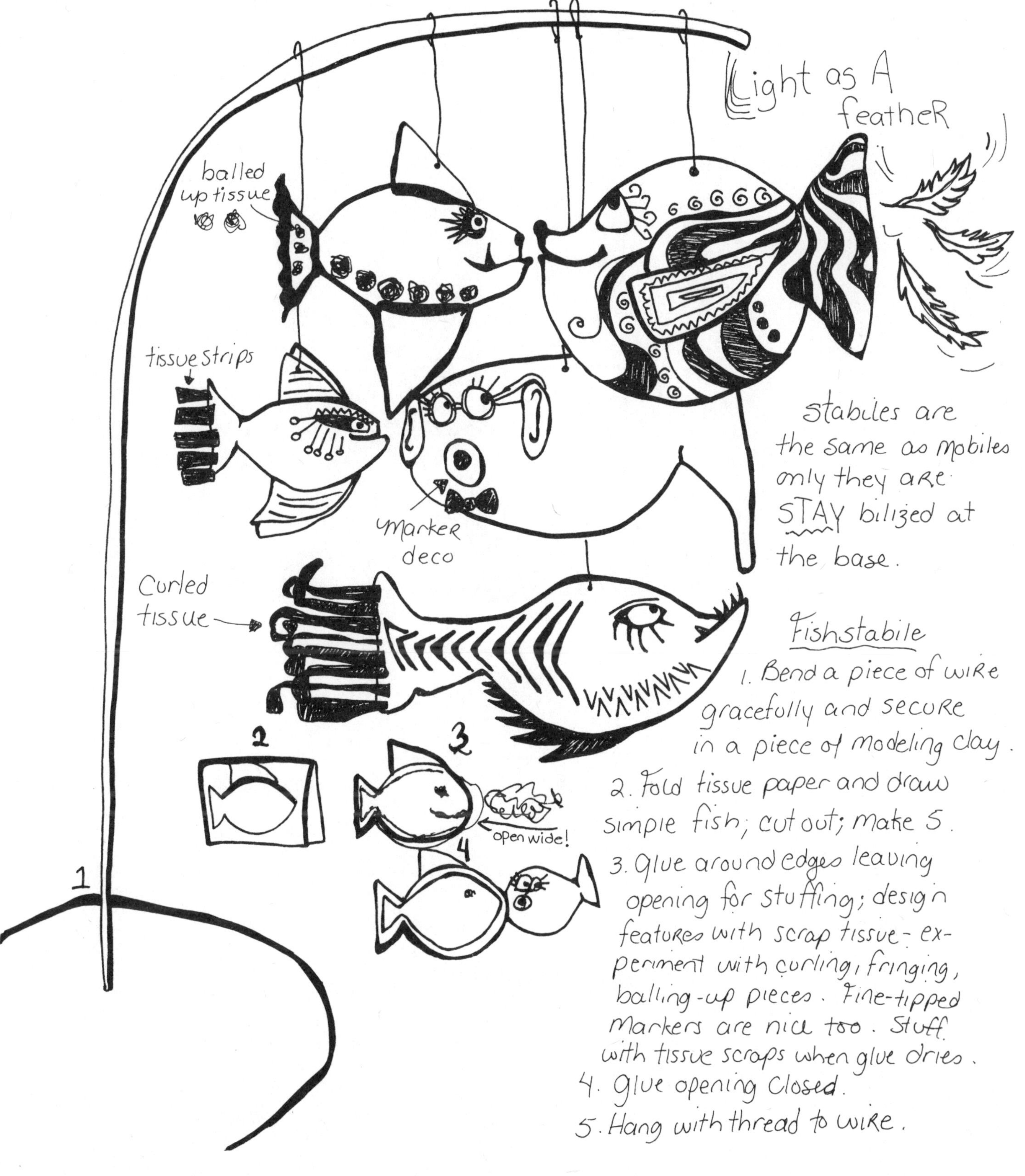

tin snowmen

START COLLECTING those tin pie plates, TV dinner trays or bakery item trays - they are perfect for metal tooling. Make a snowpeople mobile ~ deeee-lightful!!

* use 5 trays *

1. Remove rim from tin trays.
2. Place tin-aluminum, actually on a padding of newspapers and create 5 snowpeople engaging in various winter activities - skating, skiing, snowshoeing, snowball fighting, etc.
3. Keep flipping aluminum over so you get impressions on both sides of metal.
4. Carefully cut out.
5. Fold arms and legs forward and backward to achieve a feeling of animation. Glue yarn hair, scrap wool scarves, felt earmuffs and boots.
6. Pierce hole with needle and attach snowpeople to wire with nylon thread.

CELLOPHANE MOBILE

Cellophane is wonderful in suspended animation because as one form dances across the next, a new color emerges.

1. Fold 9" by 12" construction paper (black) in half + draw tree - draw a second tree within first with 3/4" margin; cut inside tree out as well as outside tree. (X-ACTO knives are helpful here.)
2. glue cellophane between 2 trees and glue both trees together.
3. With black scraps, make ornaments and glue to cellophane.
4. Punch hole on top of each tree and hang with thread to reed.

PEOPLE MOBILE

Clothesline People

ooh what fun · superstars, self-portraits, people in a circus, animals from outer space, Halloween characters, kids from foreign lands.

~ these are great to hang from a string that goes like a clothesline, from one end of the room clear to the other end; each kid makes one

– OR – each kid makes a bunch of people – one for every member of his family! ★ how's that!??

Here's How:

1. Make a paper pattern for all body parts.
2. Cut 2 of each part from felt, one of each part from cardboard.
3. Trim cardboard pieces so they're slightly smaller than felt ones.
4. Sandwich cardboard between felt + glue together.
5. Using a needle + thread, connect head, body, arms and legs.
6. with sharp, fine tipped black marker, draw in features.
7. glue on yarn hair, felt capes, belts, shoes, ties and purses.
8. Tie head with thread and string to line for group exhibit OR coat hanger for personal, individual family tree.

YARN MOBILE

Kids just love making these! Rug yarn works best, as it lays nicely when playing with shapes. Other types will do.
PICK A THEME
★ jack-o-LANTERNS
★ VAlentine hearts
★ AniMAL farm
★ Underwater trip
★ celestial scenes
★ Insect worlds
★ free form designs
1. Make a thick papier-mâché mixture or thin white glue 50-50 with water-mâché works better.
2. Dip lengths of colored yarn into mixture, squeezing off extra.- the yarn should be thoroughly saturated.
3. Lay design shapes onto a sheet of wax paper-criss cross, overlap and squiggle it!
4. When dry, suspend with yarn from dried branches or dowels.

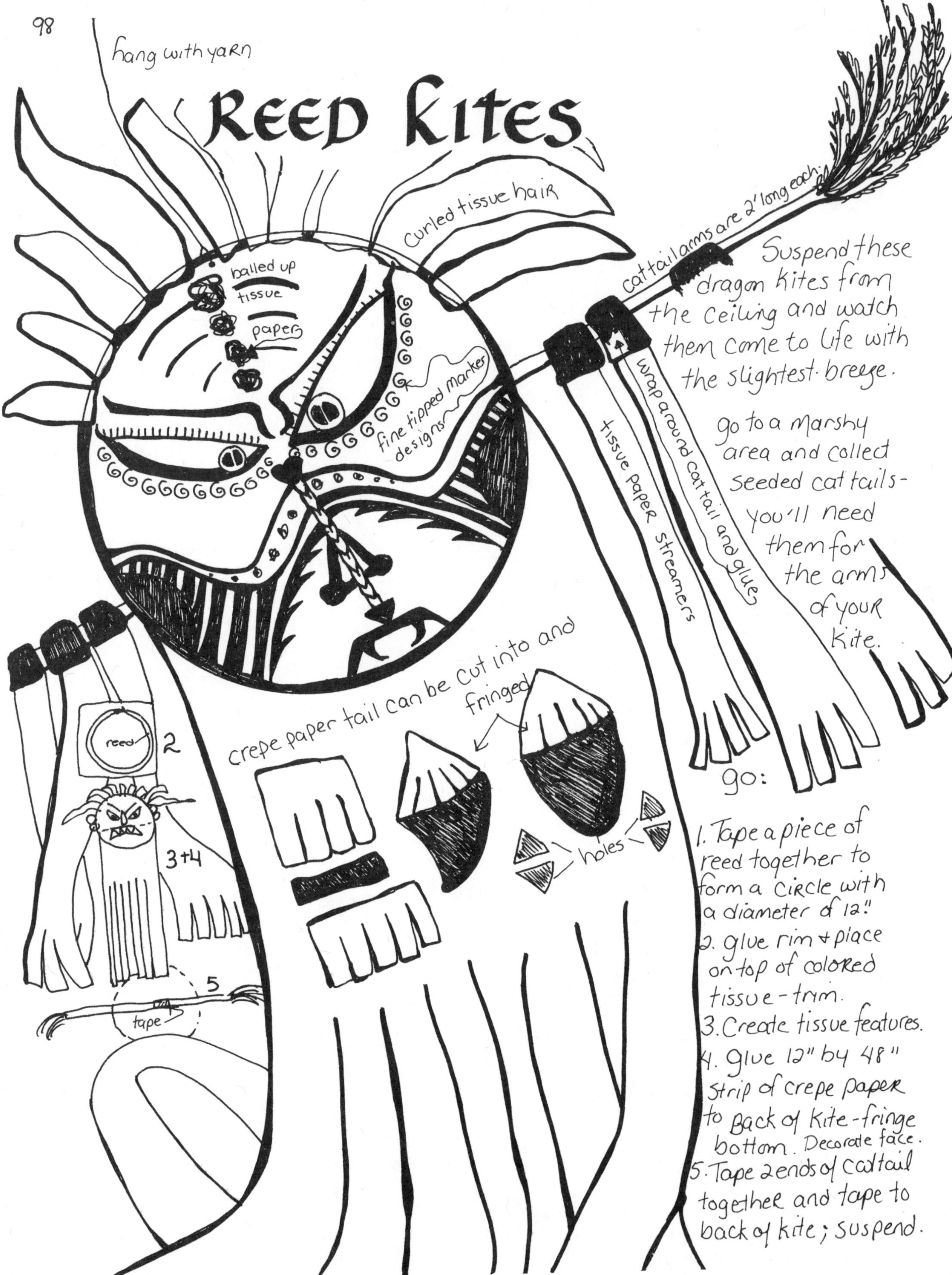
hang with yarn
Reed Kites
Curled tissue hair
cat tail arms are 2' long each.
Suspend these dragon kites from the ceiling and watch them come to life with the slightest breeze.
balled up tissue paper
fine tipped marker designs
wrap around cat tail and glue
tissue paper streamers
go to a marshy area and collect seeded cat tails - you'll need them for the arms of your kite.
crepe paper tail can be cut into and fringed
reed
2
3+4
holes
5
tape
go:
1. Tape a piece of reed together to form a circle with a diameter of 12."
2. glue rim + place on top of colored tissue - trim.
3. Create tissue features.
4. glue 12" by 48" strip of crepe paper to back of kite - fringe bottom. Decorate face.
5. Tape 2 ends of cattail together and tape to back of kite; suspend.

toothpick mobile

fig. A

Use flat toothpicks

practice without discouragement
-you'll get it!!

toothpick sculptures are a nerve-racking addiction.
- it's like pick-up sticks or making card houses.
- a matter of delicate balance, steady nerves and lots of patience. I've never met any kid who has seen a toothpick mobile who hasn't wanted to make one. I've never had a kid give up - no matter what!!!

1. Make a reed frame and use masking tape to secure. You may use a long piece of reed and loop it two or three times to make a multi-faceted form - fig. A.
2. Starting at tape, lay one toothpick down at a time - the 1st one has both ends touching the reed; each succeeding one has one end touching the reed, the other touching the toothpick.
3. Keep going around in the same direction - don't break toothpicks.
4. Keep spacing even; experiment with consistent patterning.
5. Tie to reed or suspend with string.

tin can top mobile

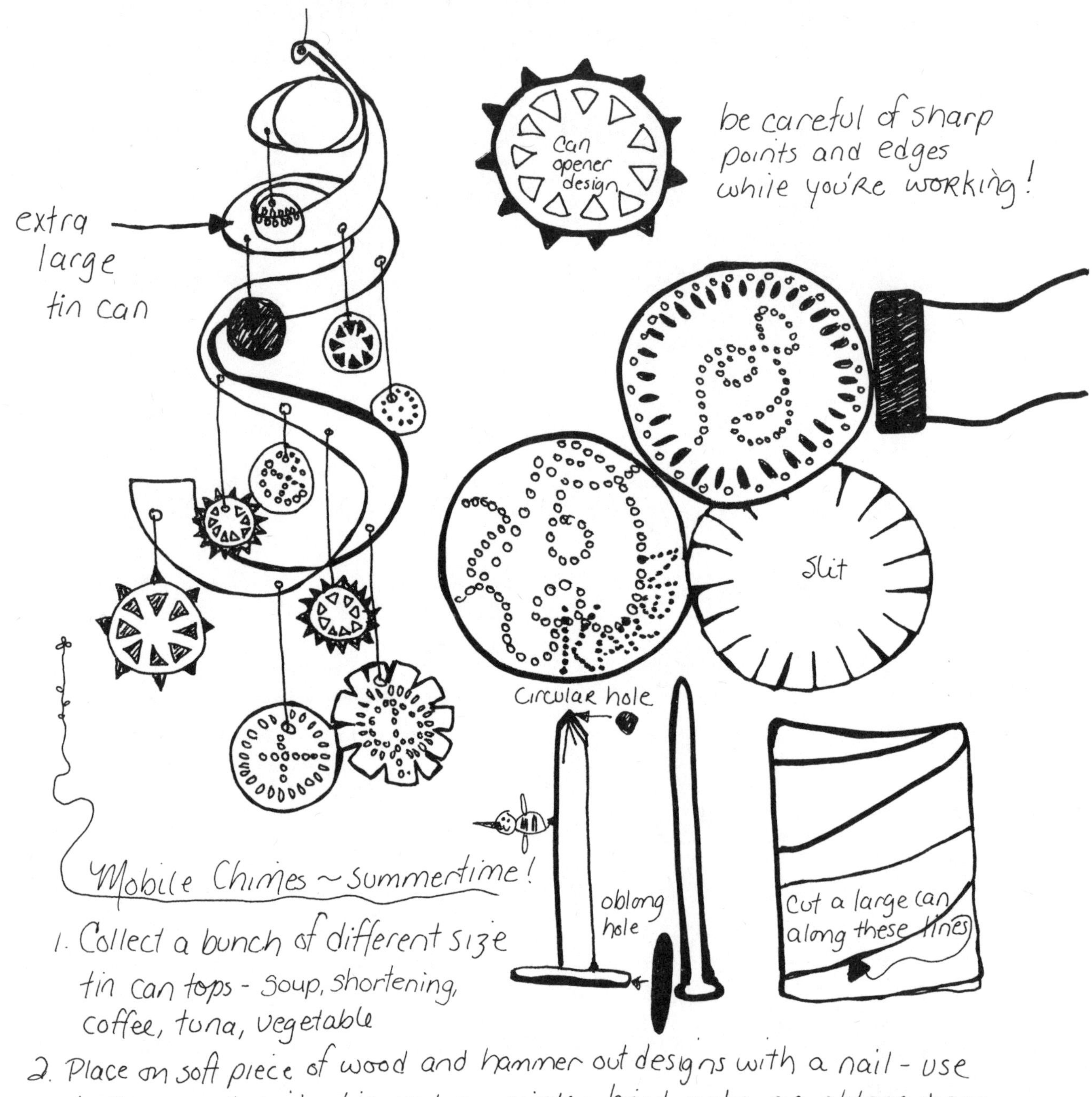

Mobile Chimes ~ summertime!

1. Collect a bunch of different size tin can tops - soup, shortening, coffee, tuna, vegetable
2. Place on soft piece of wood and hammer out designs with a nail - use both ends of nail - tip makes a circle; head makes an oblong shape.
3. Try "can-opener" shapes before removing lids from can.

OR

simply hang whole!

Use metal cutter with CARE!!!

4. Using a metal cutter, cut a can that has both ends removed in a downward spiral shape - punch holes and hang lids from spiral.

metal mobile

Make playful imaginary creatures or African animals or animal crackers from pliable wire and steel wool. (You can practice your animal shapes first by drawing them, using one continuous line on a piece of paper.)

1. Make 4 or 5 animals using one length of wire for each one. Thinner wire may be integrated for smaller additions- eyes, ears, tails and horns.
2. Use steel wool within your animal body- for manes and fur, or to create fullness in part of the shape- the belly!
3. Suspend from coat hanger with fishing line.

BIRD IN A CAGE

1. Cut 10 18" by 1" strips of black construction paper-spread out like spokes of a wheel and staple ends together.
2. Make bird by sticking toothpick into 2½" styrofoam ball, then pushing smaller styrofoam ball into remaining section of toothpick. Add tailfeathers, pipe cleaner features and crown and a beaded eye-stick a straight pin through the hole in the bead. Make some pipe cleaner legs.
3. Bring bottoms of strips together to form cage - staple shut.
4. Insert bird. Tie to top of cage. Suspend cage with fishing line.

soft art
HOWDY!
* Burlap heads *
say hello to soft art! once you get hooked on it, an avalanche of ideas will follow!
these burlap heads are a fun, simple introduction to soft, stuffed shapes ~ they may be made big for bed rest pillows or filled with beans to make wonderful bean bags!
1. Cut 2 duplicate forms (forms head + body)
*stitch at least ½" in from edge - use thin yarn.
2. • Stitch on a nose
• Use round beads or buttons for eyes
• Create a mouth - yarn or felt is great.
3. Stuff with polyfiberfill. (or beans)
4. Fringe 2 layers of felt and insert between burlap at bottom of head. Stitch all 3 layers closed.
5. Stitch (or glue) on skating legs, waving arms and tossled hair; add ribbons + bows.
felt works well
BIG HUMPTY-DUMPTY PILLOWS
OR
SMALL BEAN BAGS
(use felt instead of burlap, when making bean bags)

simple soft

★ Using two duplicate shapes of felt, a spirited mind instinctively begins to develop a myriad of excitingly creative forms. Soft art forms have no bounds; they may be suspended as mobiles, weighed down as bean bags, layered into double-decker hamburgers, inflated, deflated, combined with other art forms or simply enjoyed as a nice, soft....

apply fur, felt, yarn with glue; ornament your tree with animals!

★ experiment with fabrics.

★ if a material frays easily, however, it is best to machine sew, then turn stitching to inside.

★ The best stuffing is polyfiberfill, although cotton batting, nylon stockings, shredded foam and pillow stuffing will work fairly well.

★ Certain types of soft art require "puffy" flatness—or support. For felt, sheets of polyester batting is the best stuff! Use it between felt (cut slightly smaller) as in the angel wings on the next page.

★ for best results, stick to simple, smooth pillow forms.

★ Make a portrait pillow—of mom, pop or for your very best friend!
★ be sure to include those freckles!

suggestions

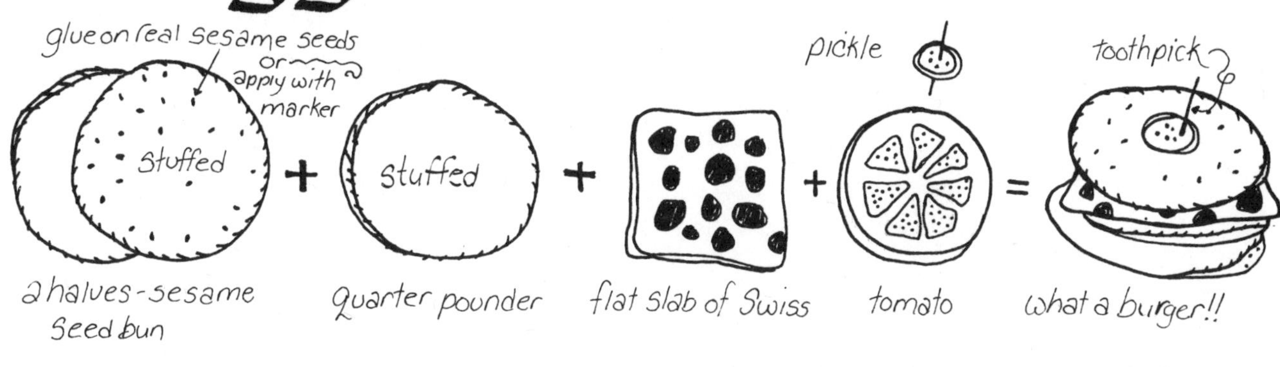

★ My friend Frank delighted me with my first quarter pounder! I'm a vegetarian and what a treat it was!!! SMACK!!!

★ The overcast stitch is recommended for finer quality soft art; it takes longer than the running (-----) stitch, but stuffs plumper, having a nicer visual effect. Keep those stitches uniform!

★ The overcast stitch may be used in combination with the running stitch for certain effects.

i.e. when using flat cotton batting between felt, an overcast is used on the perimeter and a running is used internally to delineate. Look at the wings on this chubby angel - she's really in heaven!

running stitch

overcast stitch

overcast stitch

★ Besides felt application for division of shape and color and props and features and ★ and ★ and ★ and break the monotony - please!!! Use some real stuff → seeds, shells, feathers, beads, silk flowers, ——— umhhh! ♥

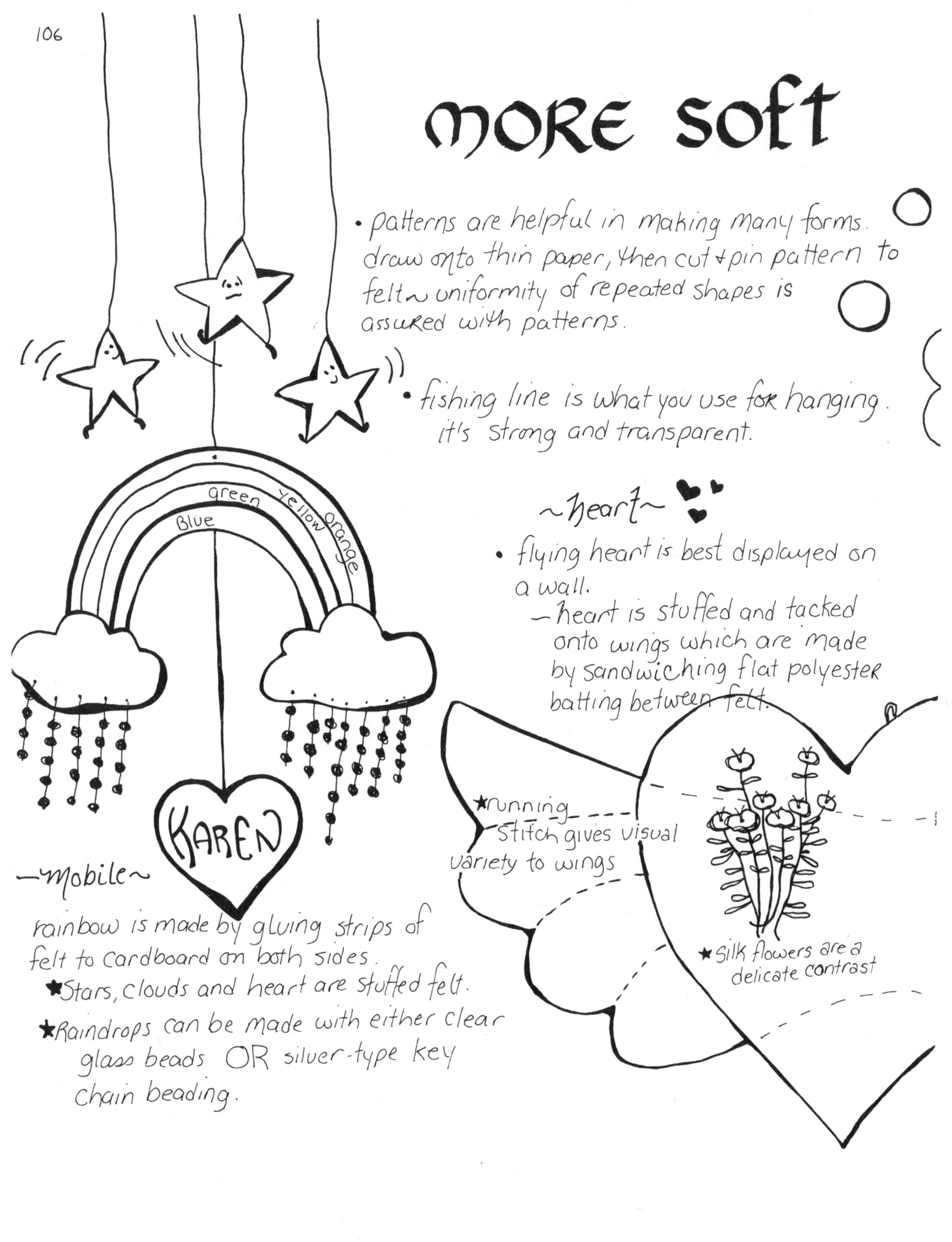
MORE SOFT
• patterns are helpful in making many forms. draw onto thin paper, then cut + pin pattern to felt ~ uniformity of repeated shapes is assured with patterns.
• fishing line is what you use for hanging. it's strong and transparent.
green
yellow
orange
Blue
~heart~
• flying heart is best displayed on a wall.
– heart is stuffed and tacked onto wings which are made by sandwiching flat polyester batting between felt.
KAREN
~mobile~
rainbow is made by gluing strips of felt to cardboard on both sides.
★Stars, clouds and heart are stuffed felt.
★Raindrops can be made with either clear glass beads OR silver-type key chain beading.
★running stitch gives visual variety to wings
★silk flowers are a delicate contrast

IDEAS

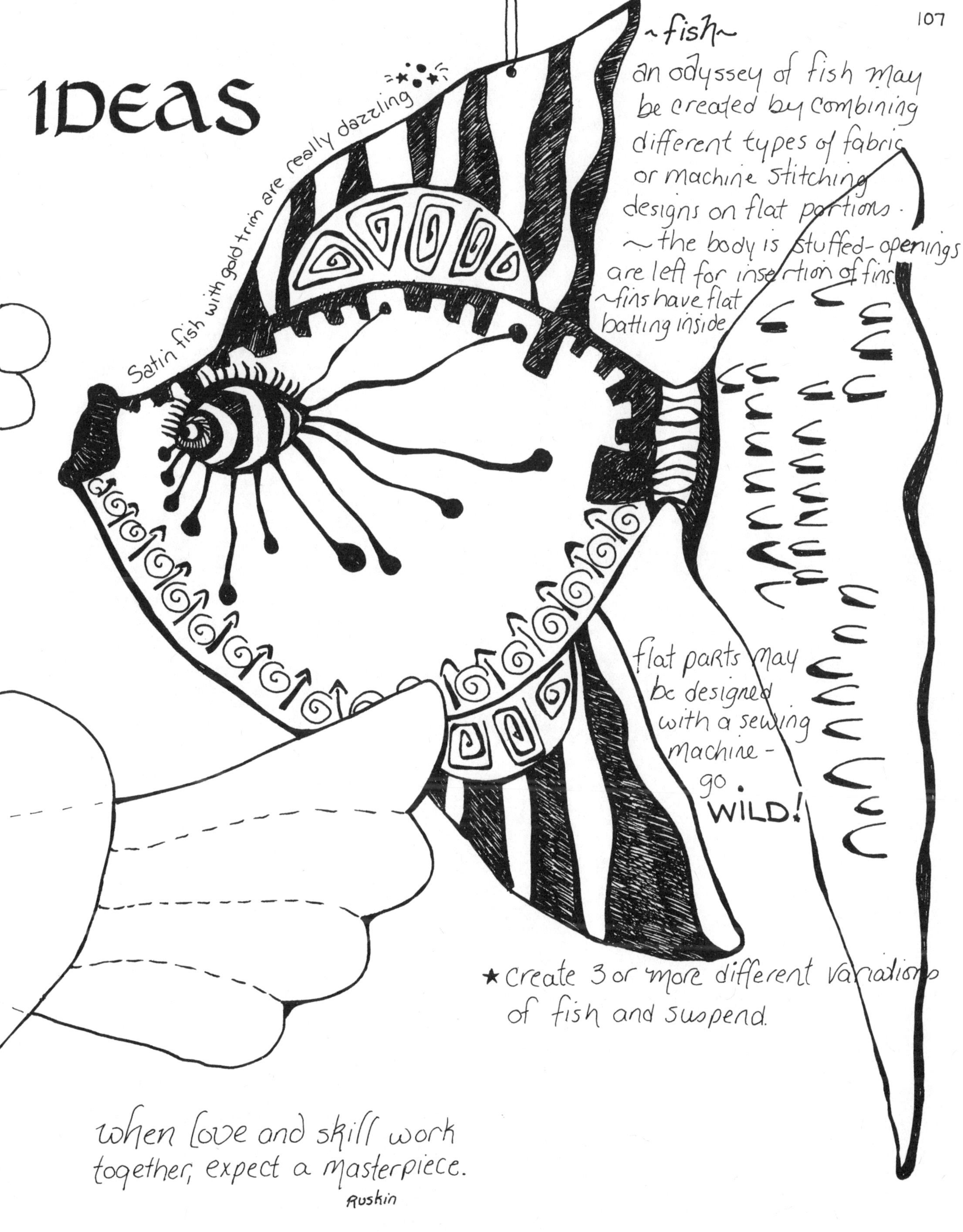

★ create 3 or more different variations of fish and suspend.

when love and skill work together, expect a masterpiece.
Ruskin

soft Lollipops

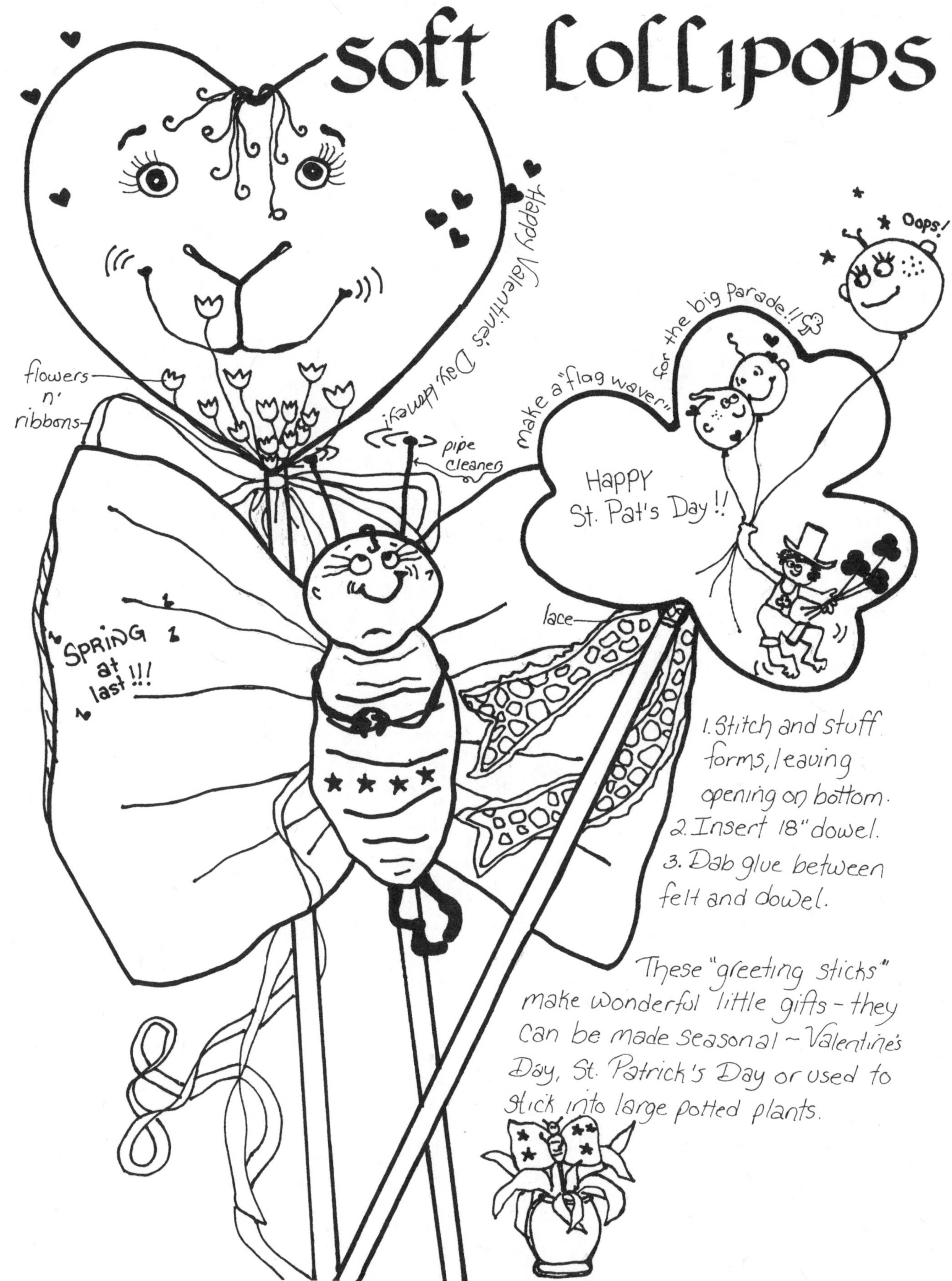

1. Stitch and stuff forms, leaving opening on bottom.
2. Insert 18" dowel.
3. Dab glue between felt and dowel.

These "greeting sticks" make wonderful little gifts - they can be made seasonal ~ Valentine's Day, St. Patrick's Day or used to stick into large potted plants.

STUFFED SAGUARO

Pronounced sa-WAH-ro, this giant cactus is found only in the state of Arizona. Many times, they live to be more than 200 years old and weigh over 3 tons! Desert birds make their homes in this state plant which blooms magnificent blossoms off the tip of the animated arms.

Potted felt saguaro

1. Cut 2 duplicate saguaro pieces from green felt. With lighter green embroidery thread, stitch cactus markings - use small running (------) stitch. Stitch both front and back of cactus.
2. Turning right sides together, machine stitch pieces together leaving ¼" seam allowance and opening at bottom.
3. Stuff with polyfiberfill from bottom of lowest arm up to top of plant.
4. Fill bottom-most section with beach sand. Stitch closed.
5. Insert cactus in clay pot; fill pot with beach sand.

★Cactus flowers may be made from felt. (or, small silk flowers are lovely!)

MUSLIN DANCERS
1
cut here
stitch here
3+4
pin, cut, divide
stitch along outside edge
5+6
turn inside out, stuff top & bottom parts; join at waist.
stitch
draw on features stockings and slippers
★ paper pattern - make body 15" tall, from head to toe _ *allow ¼" extra for seam allowance
yarn
gold braid
drawn on with markers
Stitch through elblows and knees so arms and legs will move.
1. Make a pattern for dancer by folding a paper in half and drawing half the body. Cut out.
2. Trace onto doubled piece of thick, unbleached muslin.
3. Cut, then slice body in half at waist.
4. Stitch all around each section leaving opening at waist.
5. Stuff with polyfiberfill, then hand-stitch body together. Stitch at joints.
6. Using fine, permanent markers, draw face, design stockings and slippers.
7. Using bits of fabric and lace, make a costume - slip on dancer - adjust waist by tying ribbon around to back - cinch!
8. Make hair from yarn - glue on.
DANCE
DANCE
DANCE
Make LONG arms and legs
la laah

appliqué pillows

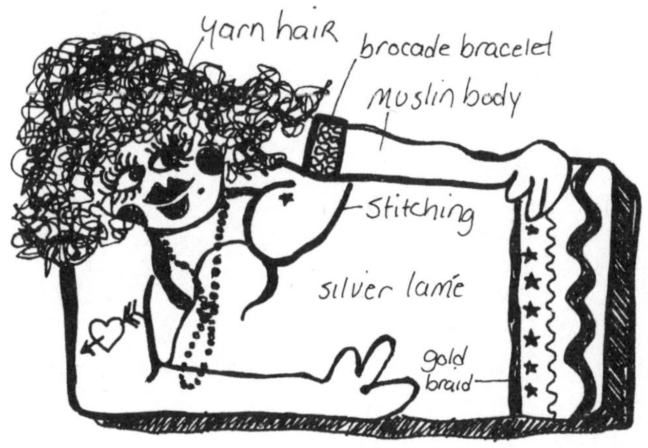

appliqué - a fabric decoration cut out and fastened to a larger piece of material.
—the New Merriam-Webster Pocket Dictionary

Soft, appliquéd pillows - a delight to behold, a comfort to weary bones.

Any substantial fabric will do - cut duplicate pieces for front and back; begin appliquéing the front with bright felts, calico cottons, muslin, poplin, duck cloth, wool or any natural fabric. Stitch, one piece at a time, to front - work large pieces in first, then finish off with detailed areas. Embellish with bits of lace, gold ribbons, ric-rac, fur or yarn. Iron flat. Turn insides of front + back together and machine stitch together, leaving an opening for stuffing. Turn outside in; stuff and hand stitch closed.

Indian fabric makes blanket

ric-rac

grey corduroy

stitched on

deep blue wool flannel

grey corduroy cut out and stitched on - vary the nap.

★ keep outside shapes simple with no sharp corners

★ bits and pieces of real jazzy fabric add spice - dig up your old New Year's Eve gown + recycle away!

(remember those gold lamés and silver brocades?!! ★★)

Burlap Pots

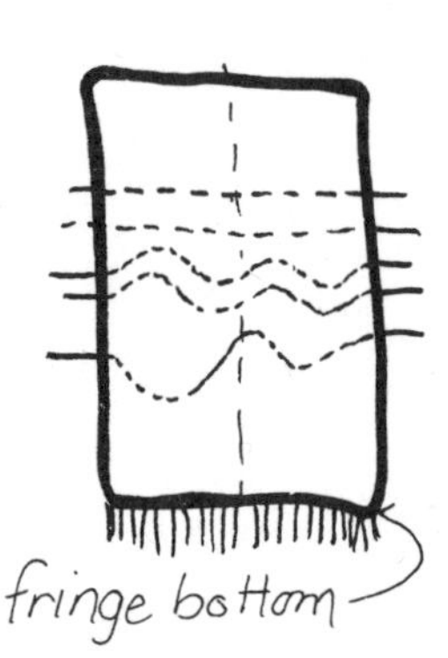

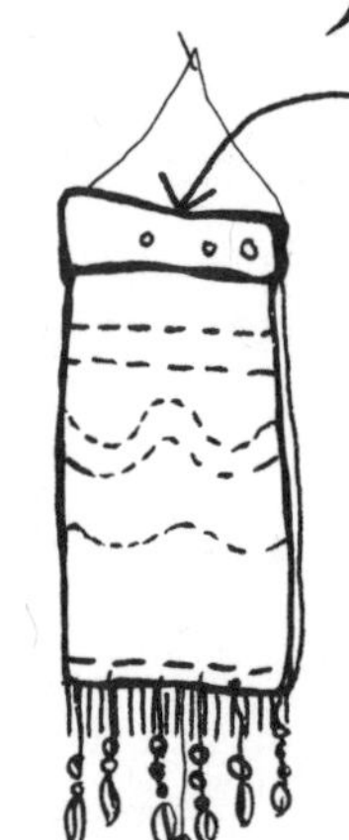

Small sand bags give weight and fullness to form.

plastic Popcorn Bag

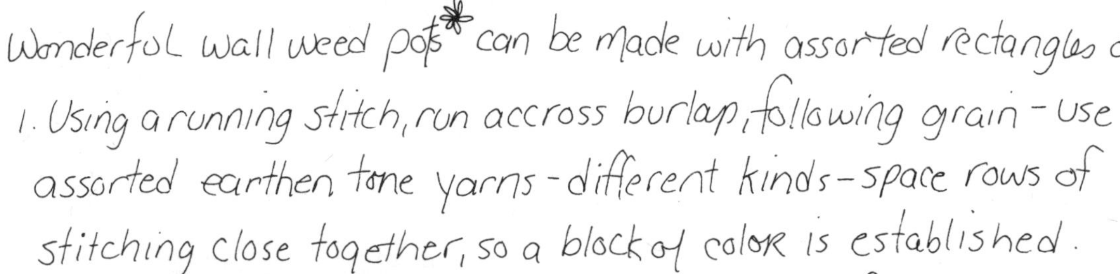

Wonderful wall weed pots* can be made with assorted rectangles of burlap.

1. Using a running stitch, run accross burlap, following grain - use assorted earthen tone yarns - different kinds - space rows of stitching close together, so a block of color is established.
2. Fold rectangle to form oblong shape.
3. Stitch along one seam and turn tube inside out — now stitch bottom closed. turn top.
4. Fill a sturdy plastic bag with beach sand + tie shut.
5. Drop sand bag into pot - it should go 1/3 the way down
6. Take a field trip and collect bunches of nature's gifts - dried weeds, grasses and flowers _ fill sacks
7. Add a few store bought straw flowers for color. Tie beads, shells and feathers to bottom.

(two or more pots can be connected)

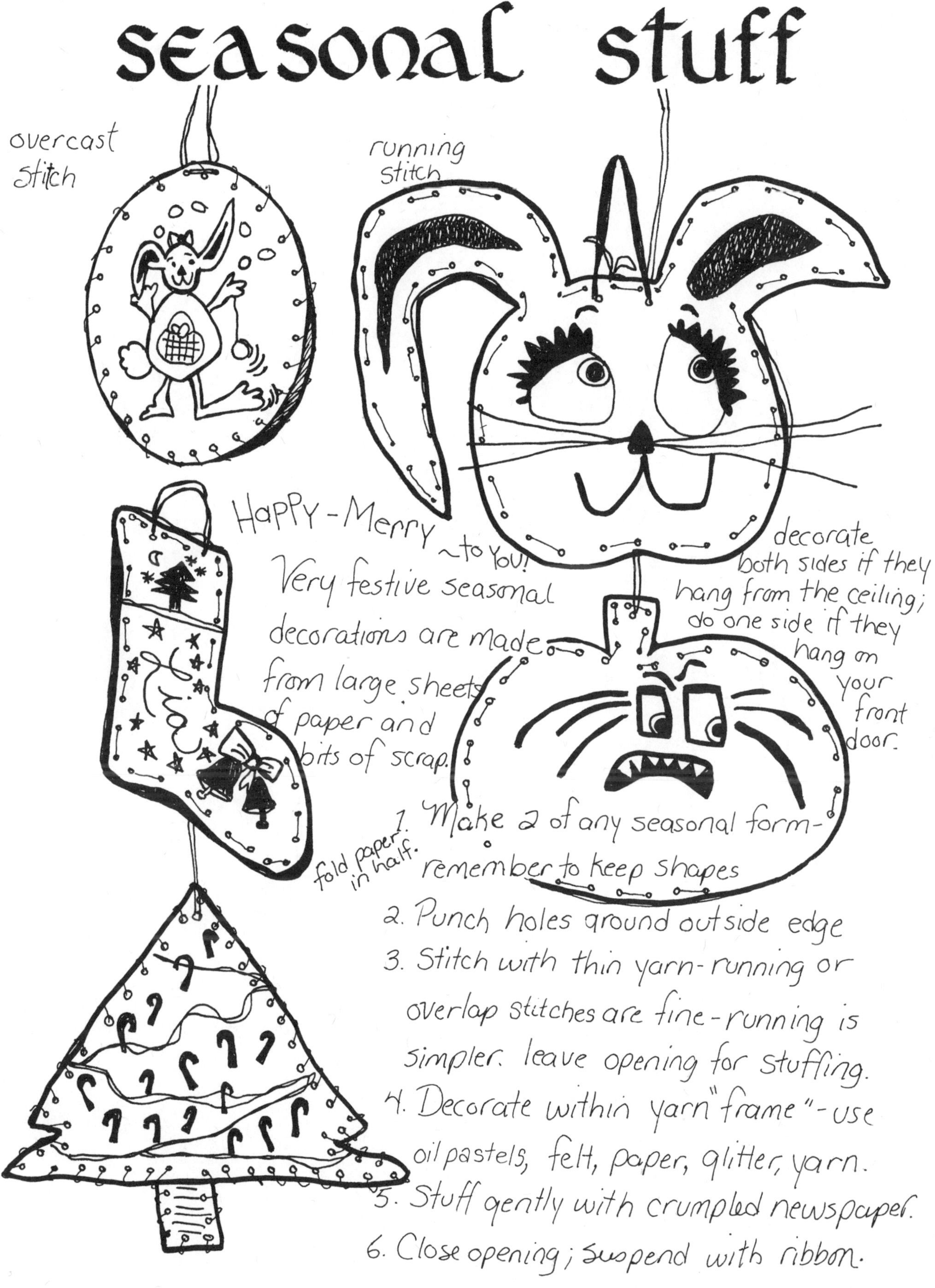
seasonal stuff
overcast stitch
running stitch
HAPPY-Merry ~to You!
Very festive seasonal decorations are made from large sheets of paper and bits of scrap.
decorate both sides if they hang from the ceiling; do one side if they hang on your front door.
fold paper in half.
1. Make 2 of any seasonal form- remember to keep shapes
2. Punch holes around outside edge
3. Stitch with thin yarn-running or overlap stitches are fine-running is simpler. leave opening for stuffing.
4. Decorate within yarn "frame"-use oil pastels, felt, paper, glitter, yarn.
5. Stuff gently with crumpled newspaper.
6. Close opening; suspend with ribbon.

BURLAP TURKEYS

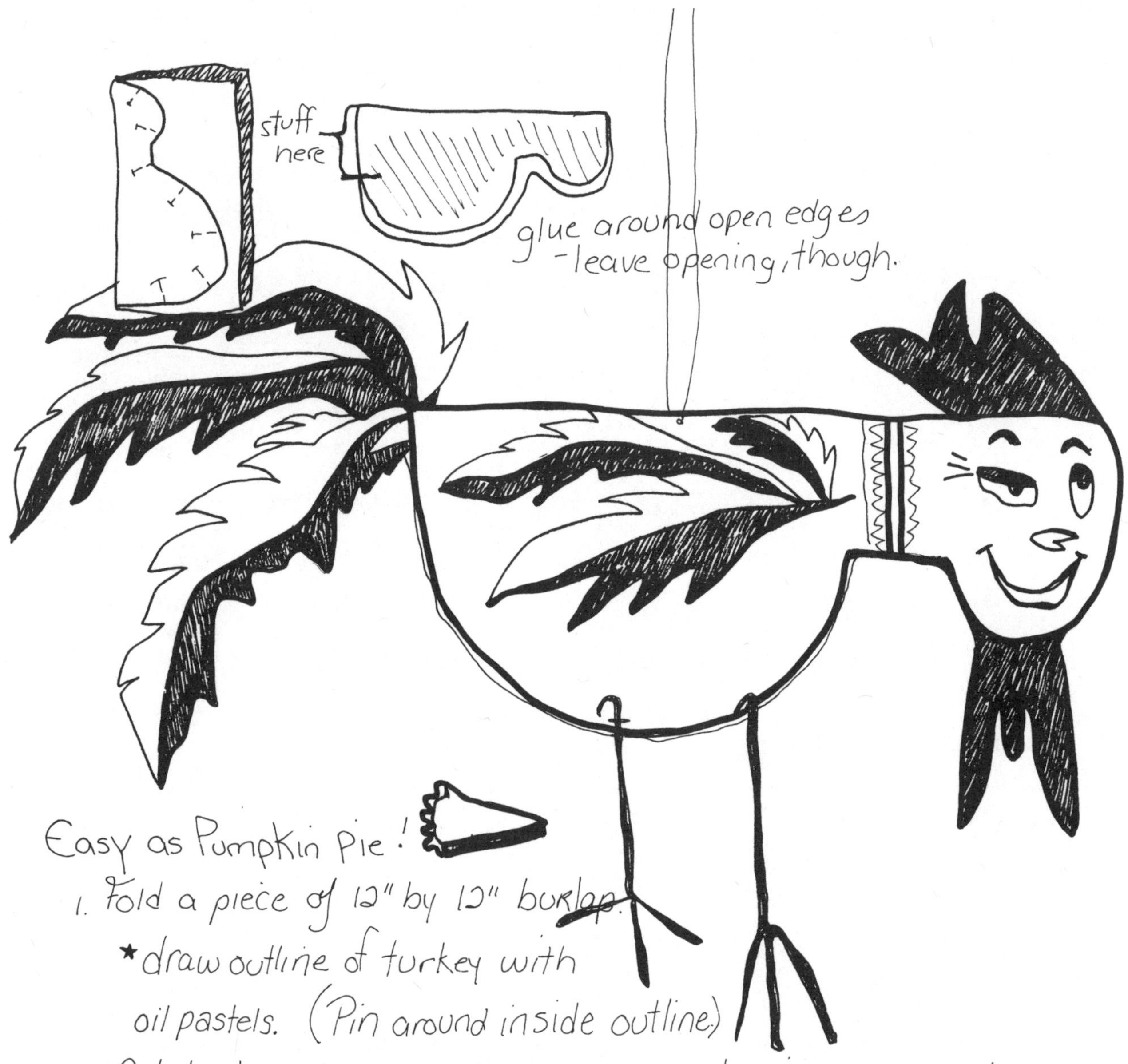

Easy as Pumpkin Pie!

1. Fold a piece of 12" by 12" burlap.
   * draw outline of turkey with oil pastels. (Pin around inside outline)
2. Cut turkey; glue around open edges, leaving an opening for stuffing; fill body with scrap fabric, nylons or polyfiberfill.
3. Glue opening shut and pin until dry.
4. Glue on tail feathers and wings - feathers may be made from colored felt. Glue on felt gobbler, comb, eyes and mouth.
5. Stitch on pipe cleaner legs; suspend with yarn.

Happy Harvest

Autumn – a time of thanks for a bountiful harvest, orange pumpkins, an odyssey of colorful trees, Halloween, Pilgrims, corn, Indians and friends. A time to

★ CELEBRATE ★

Create a spirited harvest scene for the corner of your room or entrance to your home, school lobby or Harvest Dance.

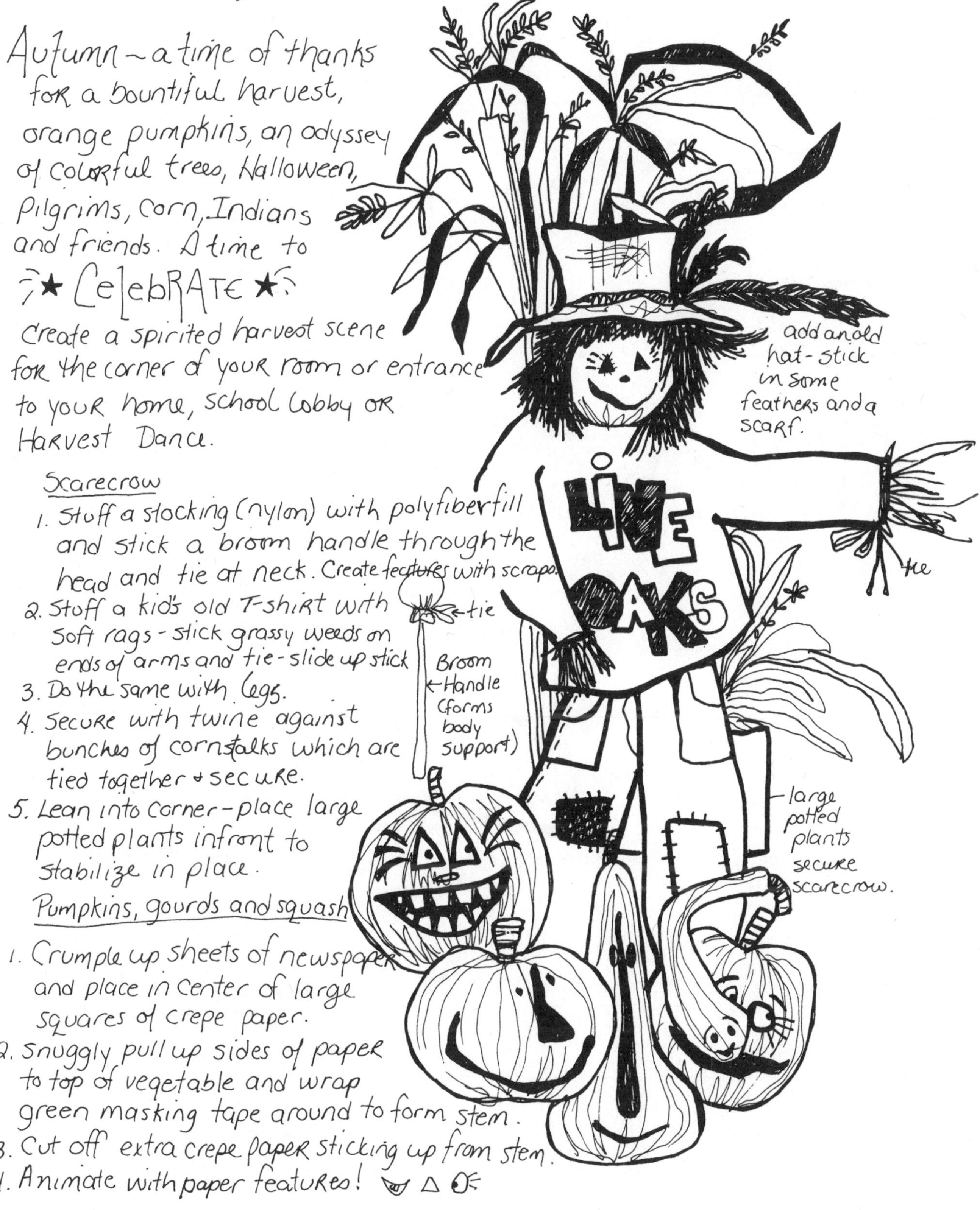

Scarecrow

1. Stuff a stocking (nylon) with polyfiberfill and stick a broom handle through the head and tie at neck. Create features with scraps.
2. Stuff a kid's old T-shirt with soft rags - stick grassy weeds on ends of arms and tie - slide up stick
3. Do the same with legs.
4. Secure with twine against bunches of cornstalks which are tied together + secure.
5. Lean into corner - place large potted plants infront to stabilize in place.

Pumpkins, gourds and squash

1. Crumple up sheets of newspaper and place in center of large squares of crepe paper.
2. Snuggly pull up sides of paper to top of vegetable and wrap green masking tape around to form stem.
3. Cut off extra crepe paper sticking up from stem.
4. Animate with paper features!

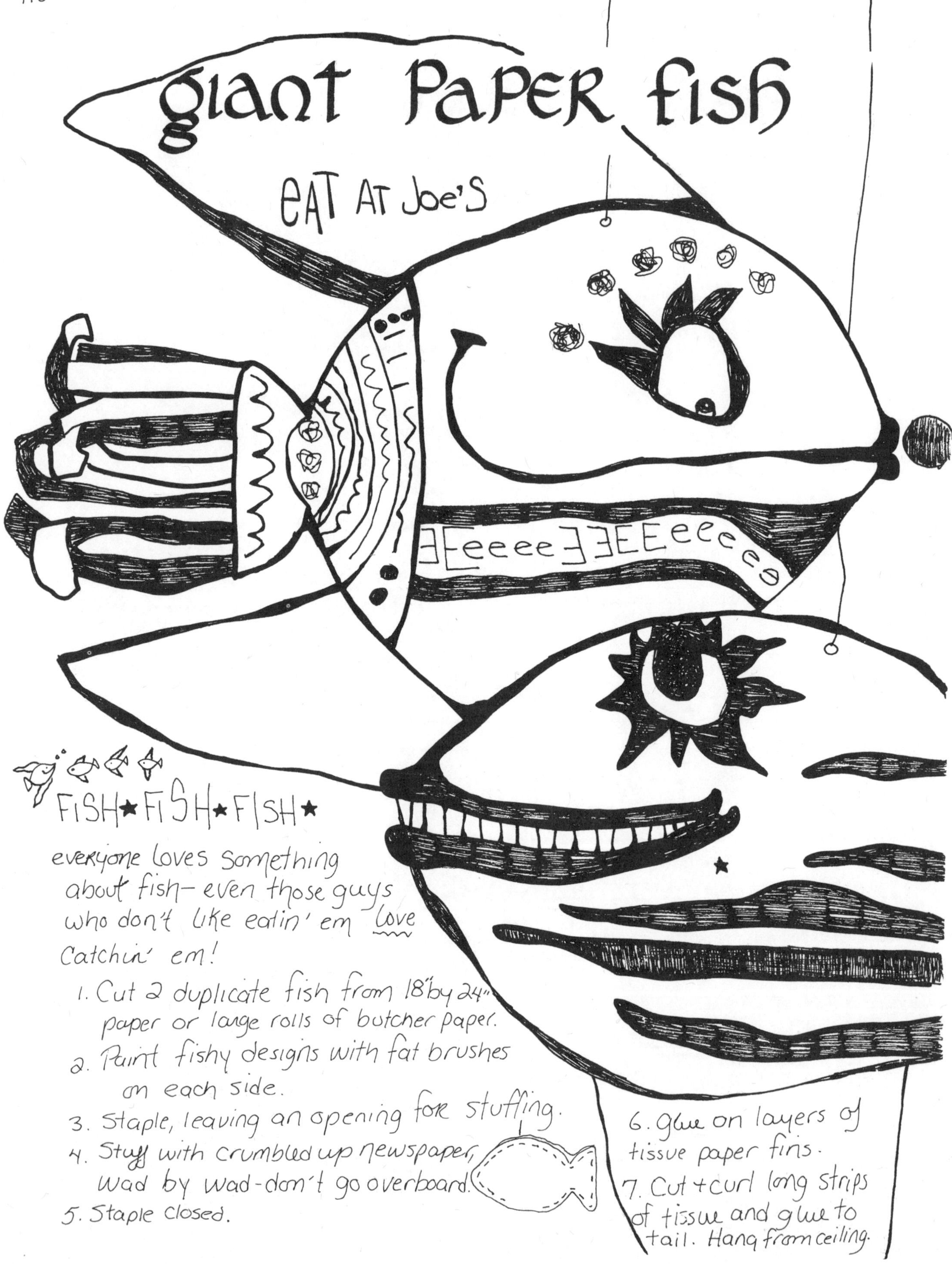

everyone loves something about fish— even those guys who don't like eatin' em love catchin' em!

1. Cut 2 duplicate fish from 18" by 24" paper or large rolls of butcher paper.
2. Paint fishy designs with fat brushes on each side.
3. Staple, leaving an opening for stuffing.
4. Stuff with crumbled up newspaper, wad by wad - don't go overboard.
5. Staple closed.
6. Glue on layers of tissue paper fins.
7. Cut + curl long strips of tissue and glue to tail. Hang from ceiling.

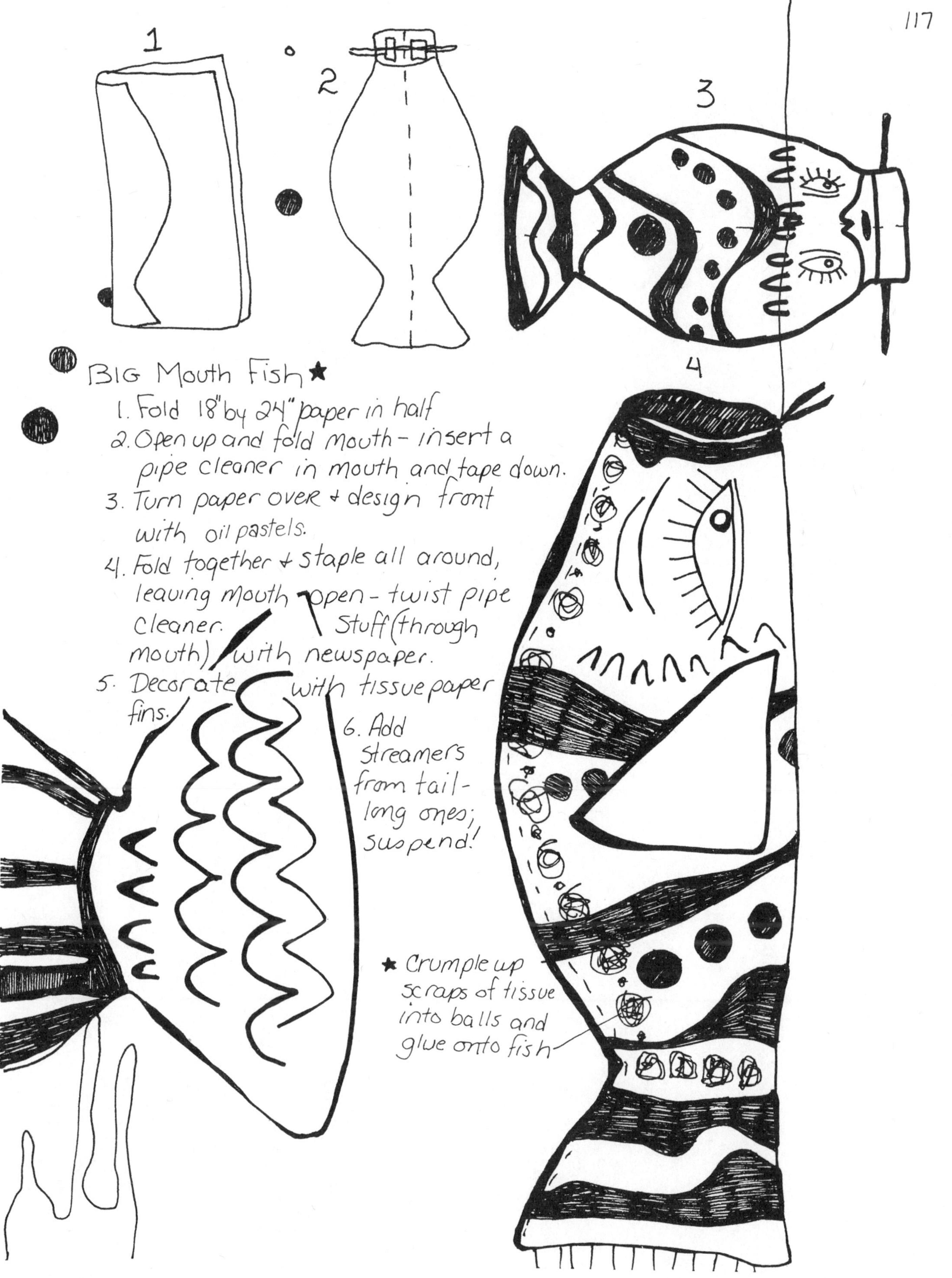
1
2
3
4
BIG Mouth Fish ★
1. Fold 18" by 24" paper in half
2. Open up and fold mouth - insert a pipe cleaner in mouth and tape down.
3. Turn paper over + design front with oil pastels.
4. Fold together + staple all around, leaving mouth open - twist pipe cleaner. Stuff (through mouth) with newspaper.
5. Decorate with tissue paper fins.
6. Add streamers from tail - long ones; suspend!
★ Crumple up scraps of tissue into balls and glue onto fish

stuff a stocking

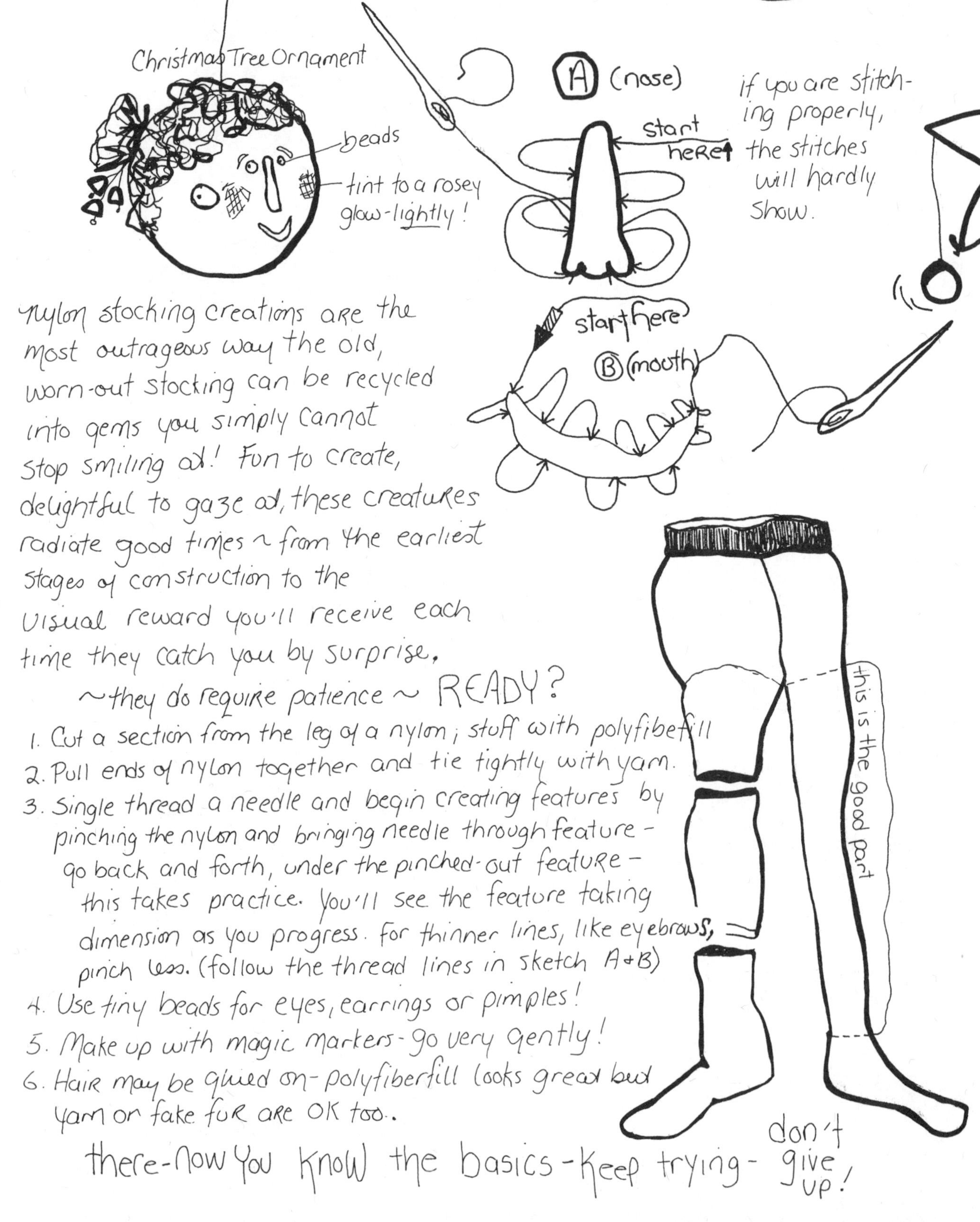

nylon stocking creations are the most outrageous way the old, worn-out stocking can be recycled into gems you simply cannot stop smiling at! Fun to create, delightful to gaze at, these creatures radiate good times ~ from the earliest stages of construction to the visual reward you'll receive each time they catch you by surprise.

~ they do require patience ~ READY?

1. Cut a section from the leg of a nylon; stuff with polyfiberfill
2. Pull ends of nylon together and tie tightly with yarn.
3. Single thread a needle and begin creating features by pinching the nylon and bringing needle through feature - go back and forth, under the pinched-out feature - this takes practice. You'll see the feature taking dimension as you progress. For thinner lines, like eyebrows, pinch less. (follow the thread lines in sketch A+B)
4. Use tiny beads for eyes, earrings or pimples!
5. Make up with magic markers - go very gently!
6. Hair may be glued on - polyfiberfill looks great but yarn or fake fur are OK too..

there - now you know the basics - keep trying - don't give up!

Kitchen Witch

as the old Norwegian story goes:
"hang her in your kitchen
an' nothing burns"- HAH!

1. Cut leg off panty hose and stuff - tie at neck + bottom to form head and body.
2. Stitch features; apply raggedy yarn hair. Apply make-up.
3. Make her a vehicle with a 12" dowel and yarn.
4. Cut doubles of boots from felt and glue to each end of 12" pipe cleaner.
5. Tie on robe + hat or scarf - use scrap fabric - roll + stuff 2 pieces of fabric for arms and stitch on.
6. Insert legs - stitch to body.
7. Attach broom - stitch arms together + tie to broom.
8. Suspend with fishing line.

these are rather flat.

Coat Hangar Faces - stretch a coat hangar into a face shape. Stretch over nylon + go · go · go ·

MOM Me DAD

tack Representatives of your loved ones to a board - barn wood looks great! Or make you and your best friend, then give it to him/her!

Stick Pins or "cognito" defense weapons for when you go jogging alone. - corsage pins work fine.

- on wood -

FAMILY PORTRAITS

- in jars -

simply stuff a head into a wide mouthed jar - for a more personal touch, add a real momento from the person you're portraying in the jar.

i.e. earrings
lace
hair
bow ties
or
freckles!

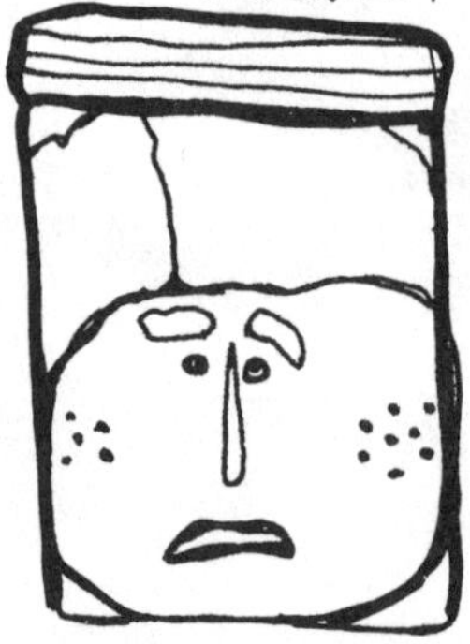

Someone let me out of here!! QUICK!!

stuffed kids

MAKE A LIFE SIZE DUMMY OF YOURSELF!

You'll need large sheets of white paper or butcher paper. Fold a piece in half and lay down on it. Have your friend trace you. Cut the outlined body out and staple all around, leaving an opening at the head. Color the front and the back, showing your own clothes. Stuff the body part (not arms and legs) with crumpled up newspaper and staple shut. Sit your double on a chair, having the legs hang off.

You can add yarn hair or make a prop -

- ★ jumprope
- ★ basket ball
- ★ dolls
- ★ popcorn

stuffed appliqué

You'll need a sewing machine for this one.

Choose you favorite animal, favorite fabrics and little odds n' ends that would bring smiles to the beholder - bits of lace, cherries from your aunt's old hat, plastic hairpins ~~~~

1. Cut a simple animal from fabric - pin to background fabric and zig-zag stitch all around form → ᴧᴧᴧᴧᴧᴧᴧᴧ.
2. Turn fabric over and cut open interior of animal - just make a slit here and there and lightly stuff with polyfiberfill.
   - the front of the animal should puff out but not bulge.
   - Stitch openings closed and back with a piece of quilted fabric the same size as your front background piece.
3. Stitch on decorative items - lace, feathers, etc. - stitch through both thicknesses.
4. Make a frame with strips of fabric covering raw edges.

easy quilt fun

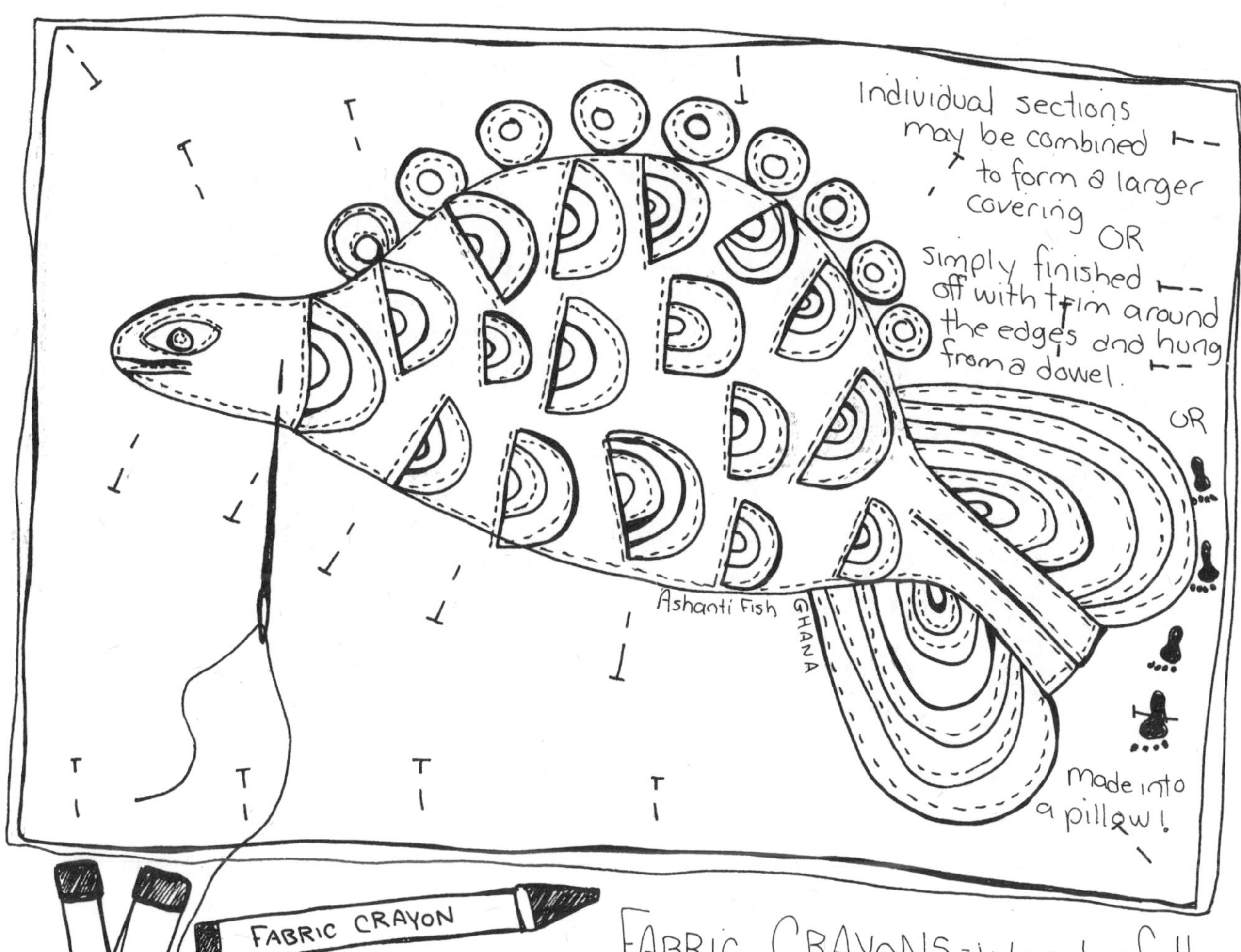

FABRIC CRAYONS-Wonderful!

fabric crayons are a terrific way to transfer colorful drawings onto cloth --- Print T-shirts, aprons, stuffed dolls or...make a quilt.

1. Draw a picture on white paper with fabric crayon.
2. Transfer picture by placing it face down over a piece of pre-washed muslin and ironing design with the setting on cotton. Iron evenly.
3. Sandwich a piece of cotton batting between the drawing and another piece of muslin the same size.
4. Pin together and stitch around image using the running stitch

Holiday stockings

Make Stockings for the whole family!

1. Draw a stocking on white paper - transfer to pre-washed muslin - follow directions for fabric crayon transfer on preceding page. Cut an identical stocking.
2. glue along outside edge of back stocking and glue front on top.
3. glue rouing to top rim to cover raw edge of stocking.
4. Write your name in glue, then sprinkle glitter over glued writing.
5. Embellish with scraps of lace, felt and trim.

STUFF with RAISINS, NUTS and POPCORN.

DRAFT SEALER SNAKES

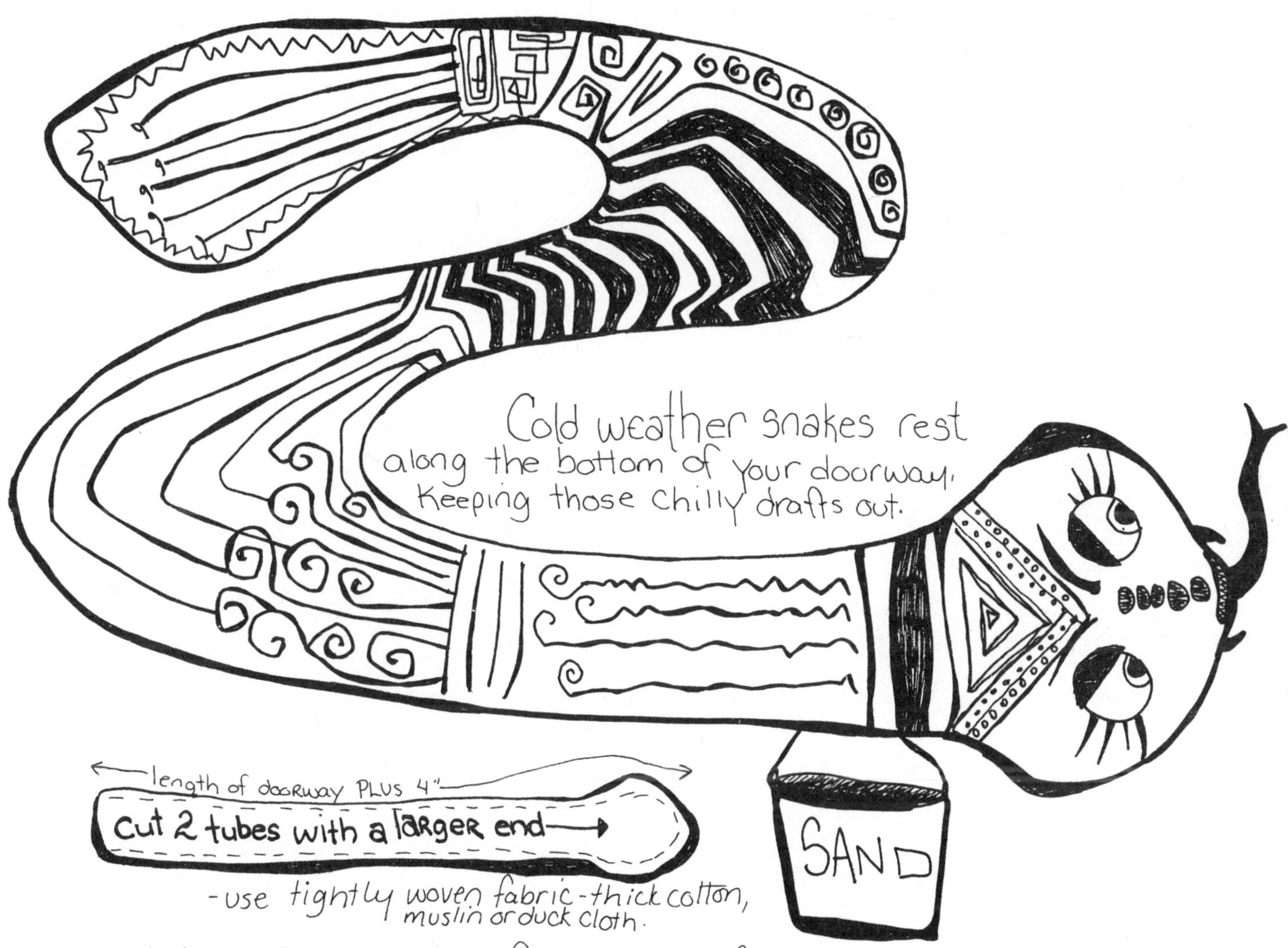

1. Measure the length of the bottom of your door way - add 4" to length.
2. Cut 2 identical snakes - 3" by length measured (including the 4")
3. Stitch both pieces together, leaving opening on end. (be sure to stitch right sides of fabrics in.) Turn inside out.
4. Fill loosely with beach sand; close opening.
5. Decorate snake's head with felt eyes, nose, tongue.

Wonderful Puppets

The enthusiasm evoked through puppetry is hardly transmittable through a crafts guide. Everyone loves puppets! Puppets lend themselves to character development, self-actualization, theatrical drama, utilization of countless skills and imaginative devices, and general, universal excitement! From felt finger puppets to ceramic marionettes, the possibilities of construction are infinite. Puppets allow an extended body for the creator and imaginations run wild! Since there are no standards for character-types, the artist is free to create totally innovative portrayals. In the midst of developing her character, the eager artist is challenged to invent original costuming, facial drama and movement in a way which encourages personal inventiveness. In addition to the pleasure derived from puppet construction, the aftermath can be equally rewarding. Puppet shows, plays and dramatizations may be used as means of exhibiting personal approaches to this individualized craft. Sharing, through drama, is especially meaningful in establishing pride and recognition from within each child and as transmitted through peer enthusiasm.

African inspired faces from Congo-Kinshasa

finger puppets I

1. Design a family group ~ one for each member of the hand ~ show that they are related ≷ OR ≶ ~ create a broadway cast from your favorite play or rock group.
2. Stitch 2 pieces of felt together on 3 sides (felt should fit comfortably around the finger ~ about 3" by 1")
3. Cut head from felt - large enough to extend beyond the edges of the tube.
4. Apply hair, headgear, features and costumes with glue, using odds n' ends ~ ric-rac, yarn, beads, sequins, feathers and fur.

finger puppets II

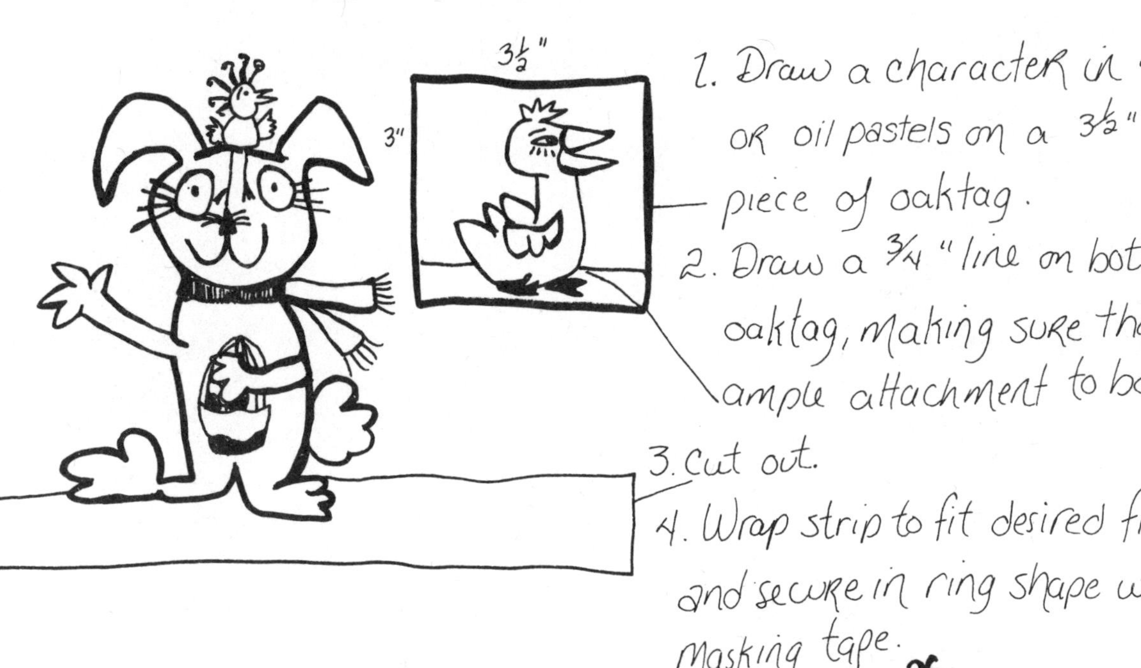

1. Draw a character in markers or oil pastels on a 3½" by 3" piece of oaktag.
2. Draw a ¾" line on bottom of oaktag, making sure there's ample attachment to body
3. Cut out.
4. Wrap strip to fit desired finger and secure in ring shape with masking tape.

bits of lace, ribbon and fabric may be glued to these puppets to authenticate costumes.

Hand Puppets

Make a portrait of your pet puppet!

1. On 2 pieces of 7" by 9" felt draw your puppet shape, leaving enough room for seams
2. Pin and cut.
3. Stitch around outside edge.
4. Raid the scrap box
   - ~peanut shell noses
   - ~pistachio finger nails
   - ~lima bean teeth
   - ~yarn hair
   - ~bow tie
   - ~neck tie

Variation: use vinyl covered wall paper instead of felt for body - nice, futuristic effect!

arm puppets

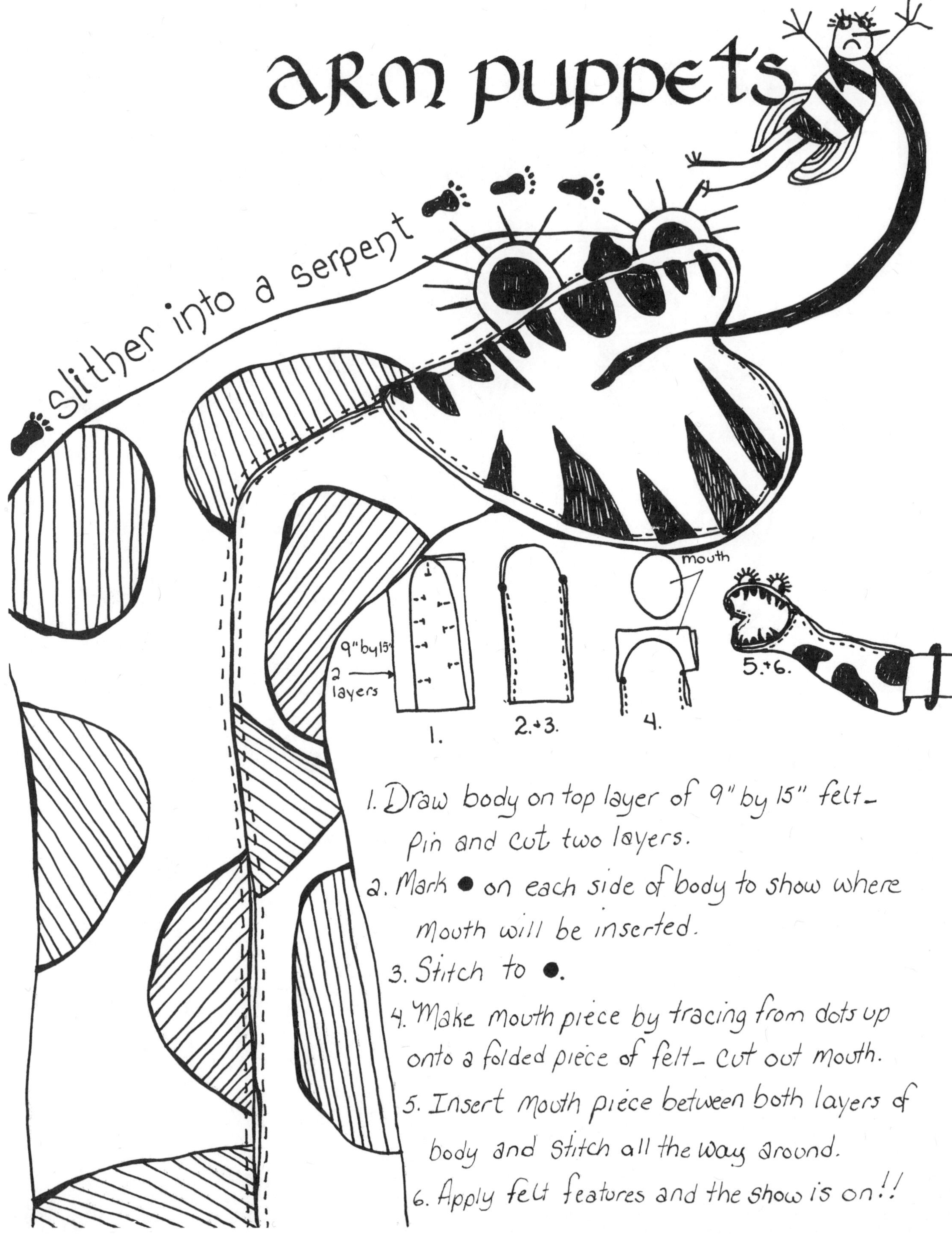

1. Draw body on top layer of 9" by 15" felt–pin and cut two layers.
2. Mark ● on each side of body to show where mouth will be inserted.
3. Stitch to ●.
4. Make mouth piece by tracing from dots up onto a folded piece of felt– cut out mouth.
5. Insert mouth piece between both layers of body and stitch all the way around.
6. Apply felt features and the show is on!!

Plate Puppets

OPEN WIDE

1. to make mouth, fold 2 paper plates in half; cut one down the center
2. Staple both plates together - hand goes in opening slits to flap the mouth.
3. Connect long construction paper body to back of puppet, just beneath bottom mouth slit.
4. Develop a character, embellish with yarn, tissue and crepe papers. Oil pastels show up nicely over construction paper body.

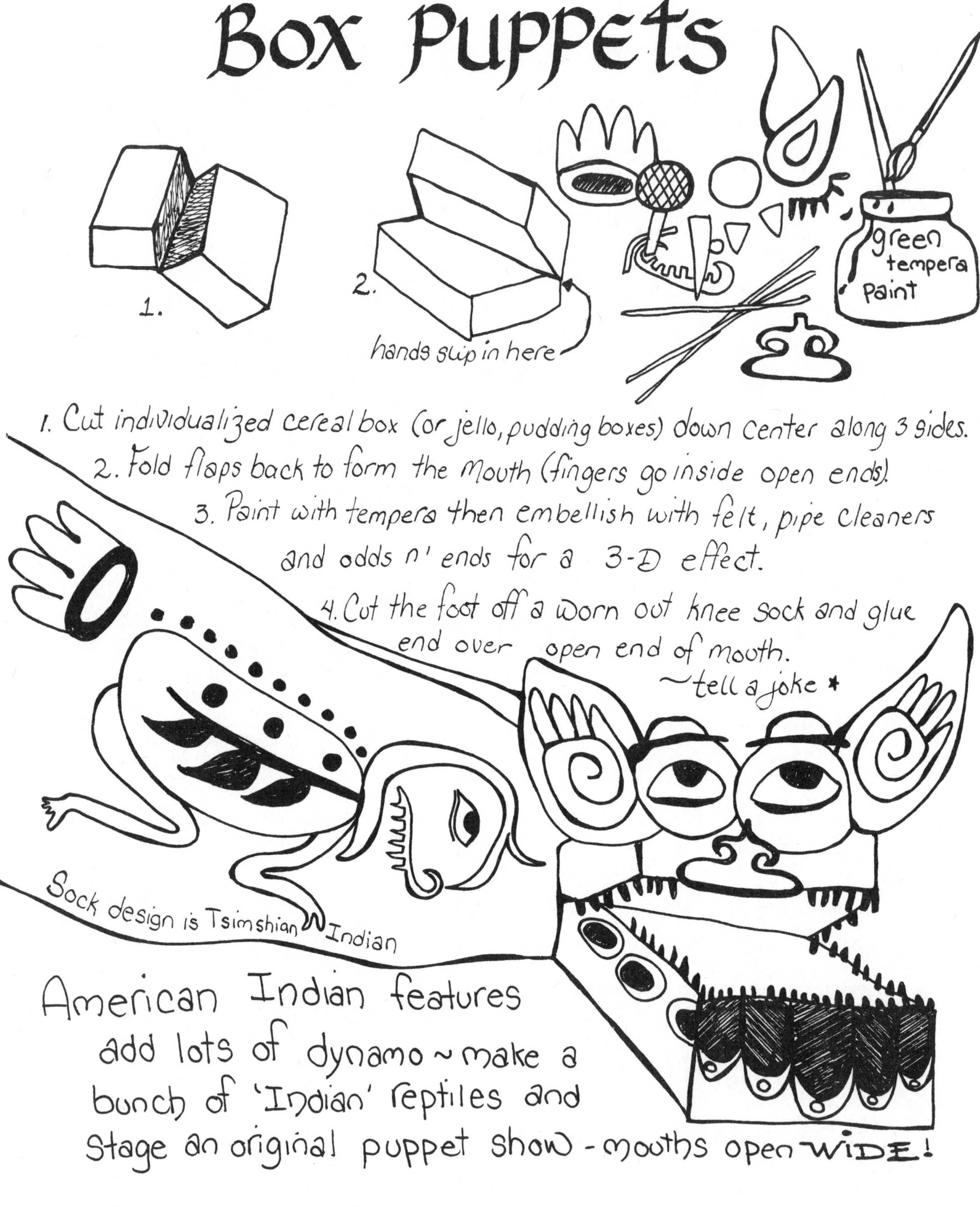
Box Puppets
1.
2.
hands slip in here
green tempera paint
1. Cut individualized cereal box (or jello, pudding boxes) down center along 3 sides.
2. Fold flaps back to form the mouth (fingers go inside open ends).
3. Paint with tempera then embellish with felt, pipe cleaners and odds n' ends for a 3-D effect.
4. Cut the foot off a worn out knee sock and glue end over open end of mouth.
~tell a joke *
Sock design is Tsimshian Indian
American Indian features add lots of dynamo ~ make a bunch of 'Indian' reptiles and stage an original puppet show - mouths open WIDE!

Flat Bag Puppets

Save those brown paper bags!! any size will work, but lunch bags work most comfortably.

1. Using oil pastels and assorted scraps, design a character for the new children's TV show!!
2. Experiment with paper to create 3-D effects on face and costume.

~ it can be:

- accordian folded
- curled round a pencil
- balled up
- spiraled — great pop-out eyes!
- looped
- fringed — great beards, eyelashes!

3. Cut and glue long arms and legs to body
4. Slip your hand inside and make that baggie chatter!

stuffed Bag puppets

1. Decorate a puppet face using smooth side of brown paper bag - use various paper techniques and yarn scraps for 3-D effects
2. Stuff bag with newspaper and insert rolled newspaper tube ~ tie at neck.
3. Using large lengths of crepe paper, wrap and gather around neck, covering chin area somewhat ~ tie with roving.
4. Apply arms and legs from strips of felt.

Envelope Chumps

Such a simple way to start a play - it's always more fun to make puppets with other people - not only do you have a cast then ~ Treasure Island, but you get to exchange a wealth of ideas from the brainstorming emerging everywhere!

1. Cut an envelope in half - glue flap.
2. Using construction paper and oil pastels create a most vivid character - cut out - be sure head is large enough to nearly cover the face of the envelope.
3. Glue to envelope, opening downward.
4. Trim with scraps - beady eyes, tin foil hooks, toothpick legs.
5. Slip your hand in and begin!!

wallpaper folk

★ Vinyl Hand Mitten ★ ★ ★ ★

a great way to teach kids the overcast stitch!

1. Pin 2 pieces of vinyl wallpaper together - wrong sides in.
2. Draw large U-shape + cut out; pin together.
3. Punch holes ½" away from edge of mitt.
4. Using fat-eyed needle and yarn stitch through first hole on bottom and knot. Then go around side to "under hole and up and around to under" again.
5. Glue on bold felt features, bows, freckles, lashes and hats.
6. Stick in your hand and go!!

★ these chaps can be made from any sturdy paper, but vinyl is final + special + nice!

stick puppets

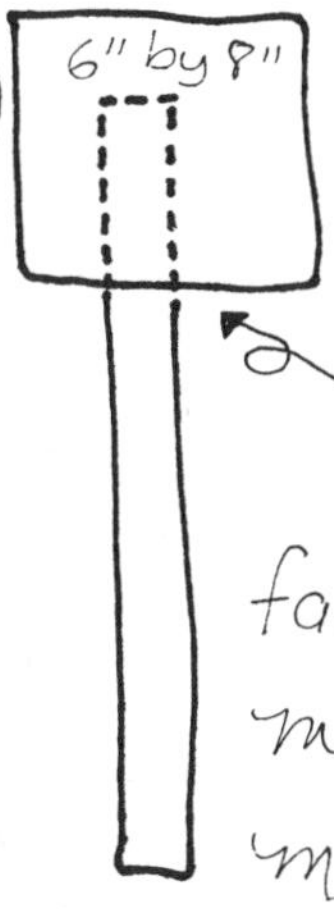

Use corrugated cardboard to create these dancin' dolls. Glue a rectangular piece of cardboard to a 24" long vertical strip.

★ Glue on thick yarn hair, felt facial expressions to create a musical facade ... turn on some music yourself to get the feeling!

★ Create a costume with construction paper embellished with scrap-box treasures.

★ attach long, free-moving arms and action legs made from paper designed with oil pastels and bits of yarn.... experiment with roving - a thick yarn!

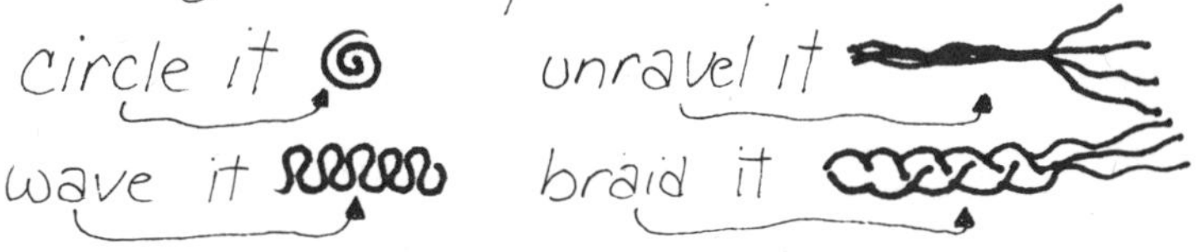

circle it — unravel it
wave it — braid it

★ A variation of these puppets may be made by using dowels inserted into styrofoam balls. Pipe cleaners, feathers, yarn, etc bring these critters to life!

Balloon Heads

celebrate the arrival of spring~ create animated heads developed from balloon inspired shapes.

Dig up: assorted balloons, thin dowels, ribbon, markers, tape, odds n' ends - scrap tissue, yarn, crepe paper ~ and Song

delight in the festivities evoked by spring ~ Maypole street songs, dancing with bare feet on soft grass, new growth popping up everywhere, bursting with color and fragrance - ummh!

1. Inflate balloon and study for characterization
2. Indulge in the creation of an animated entry for the spring parade ~ crepe paper hair, yarn grins, tissue teeth ~ some features may be applied with markers.
3. Tape balloon to dowel
4. Smile hard and parade these delights around the school!

Popsicle stick veggies

An animated Vegetable garden
A natural delight!!!

make a bunch of veggie folk from construction paper heads glued to popsicle sticks. Make your veggies come to life by giving them human characteristics – arms, legs, smiles, leaf hairstyles.

Color with oil pastels - they show up brightly on construction paper.

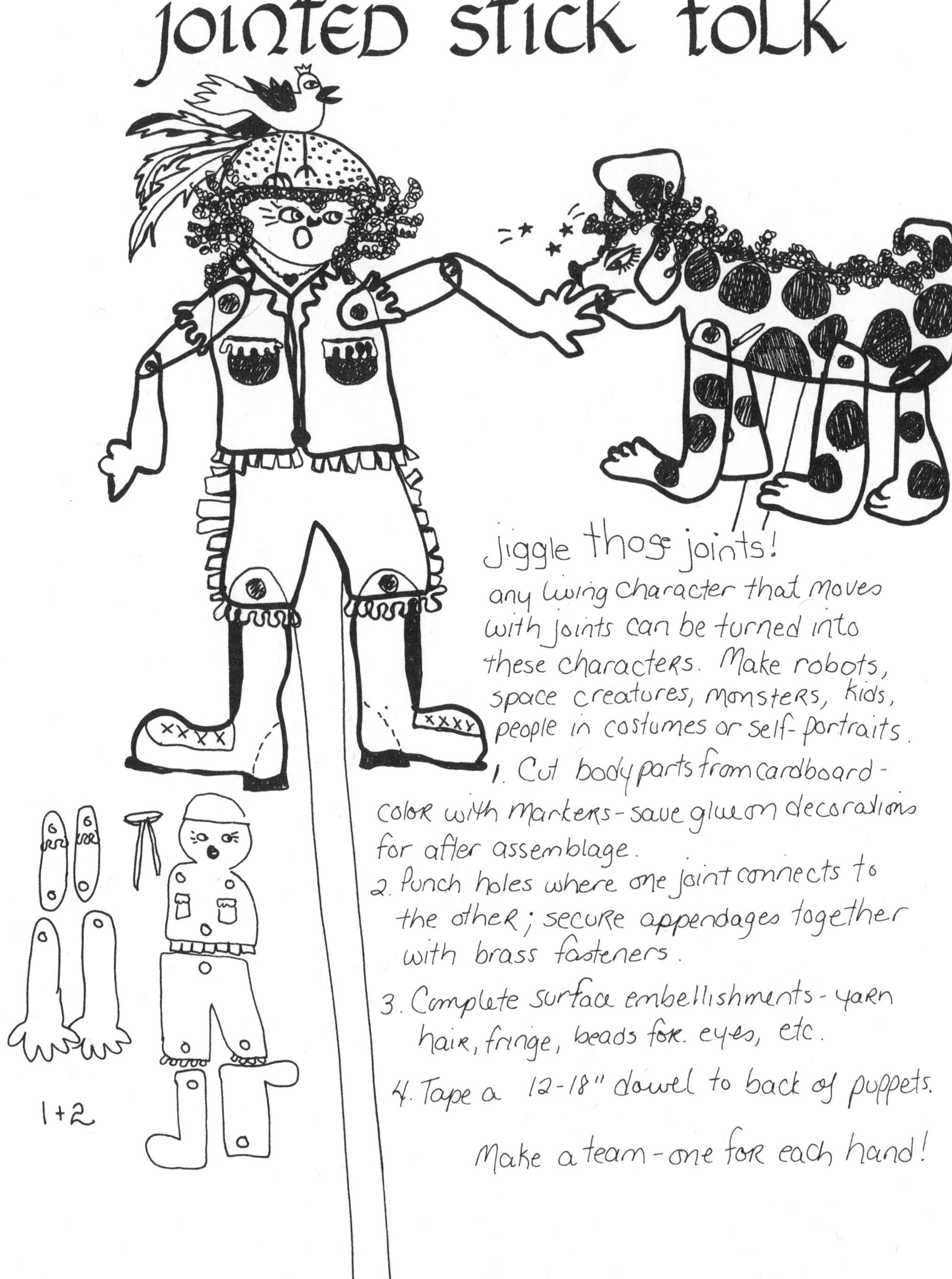
Jointed Stick Folk
Jiggle those joints!
any living character that moves with joints can be turned into these characters. Make robots, space creatures, monsters, kids, people in costumes or self-portraits.
1. Cut body parts from cardboard - color with markers - save glue on decorations for after assemblage.
2. Punch holes where one joint connects to the other; secure appendages together with brass fasteners.
3. Complete surface embellishments - yarn hair, fringe, beads for eyes, etc.
4. Tape a 12-18" dowel to back of puppets.
Make a team - one for each hand!
1+2

Rolled Tissue Puppets

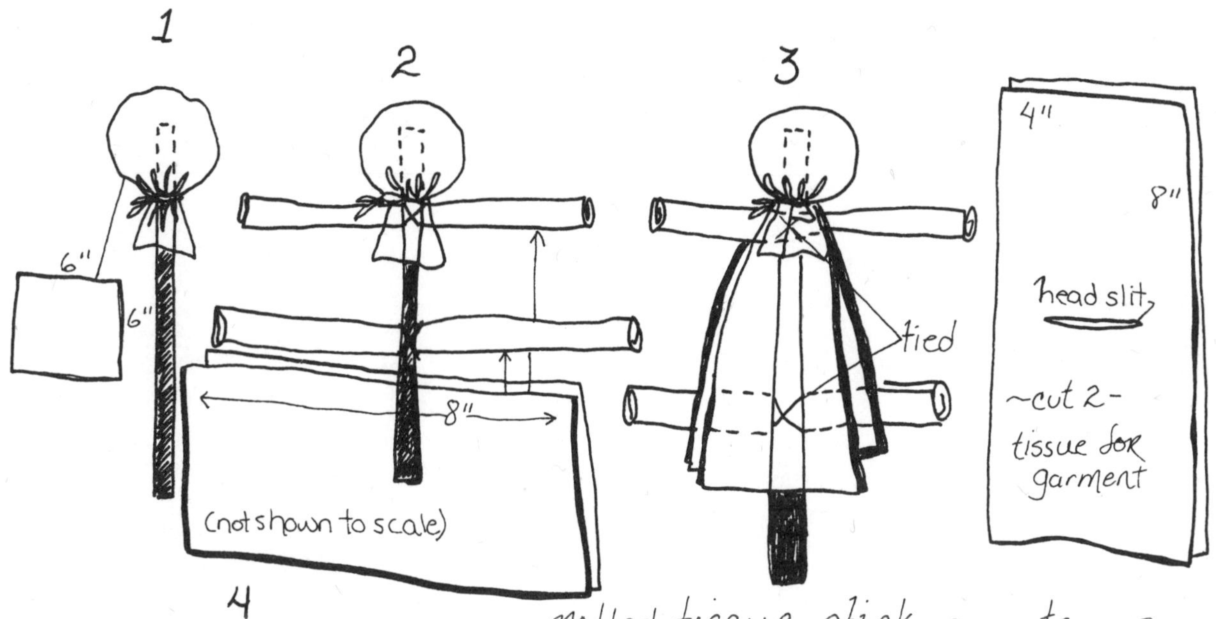

4

bodice stuffed with tissue

rolled tissue stick puppets are a variation of the corn-husk dolls which delighted Colonial children ages ago.

1. Wrap a 6" square piece of colored tissue paper over a golf-ball sized wad of newspaper which is wrapped over a 12" dowel.
2. Roll 2 sets of tissue paper - 8" square into thumb-thickness ~ tie one roll beneath neck for arms and one roll beneath waist for legs
3. Cut 2 sheets of tissue 4" by 8" for garment; drape over head through head slit;
4. Fold down legs and arms; stuff bodice with scrap tissue and tie at waist. Create features from felt, hair from yarn and a scarf and apron.

HOBBY HORSES

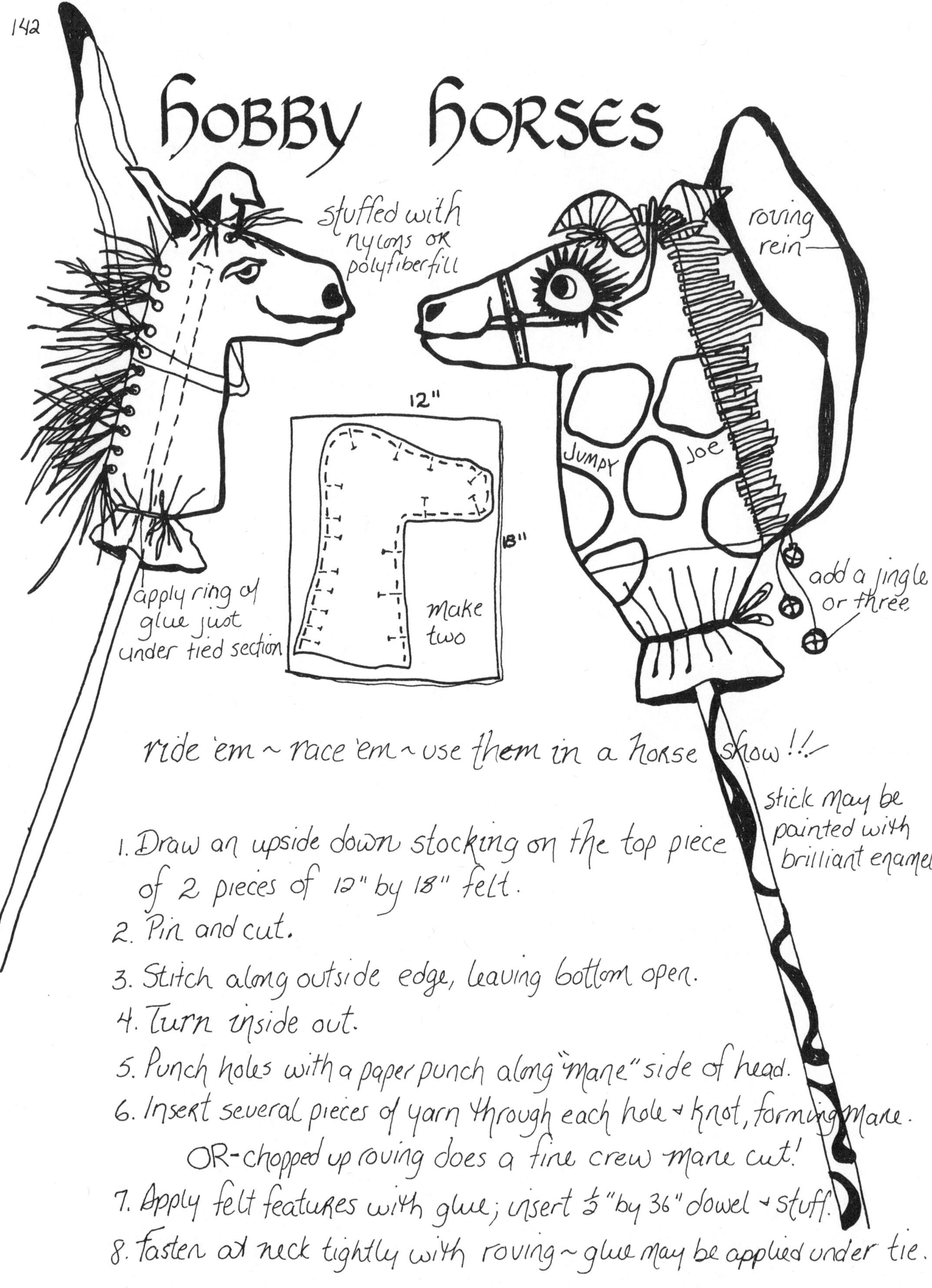

ride 'em ~ race 'em ~ use them in a horse show!!

1. Draw an upside down stocking on the top piece of 2 pieces of 12" by 18" felt.
2. Pin and cut.
3. Stitch along outside edge, leaving bottom open.
4. Turn inside out.
5. Punch holes with a paper punch along "mane" side of head.
6. Insert several pieces of yarn through each hole + knot, forming mane.
   OR-chopped up roving does a fine crew mane cut!
7. Apply felt features with glue; insert ½" by 36" dowel + stuff.
8. Fasten at neck tightly with roving ~ glue may be applied under tie.

Bottle Heads

RAINY SATURDAY AFTERNOOOOON - nothin' to do ho hum. ZZZ make some whimsy float into your day with these dancing partners. Turn on the radio and shuffle those feet!

1 Stick a dowel or broom handle in an empty plastic detergent bottle - secure with tape - either inside, outside or both, depending on the fit.

2. Dig up yarn or an old mop and glue on a hairstyle - tie bows with cut-up calico granny dresses or stick cloth flowers from old hats in her hair. Pin on a cap!!

3. Get some scraps - felt, buttons, beads, fur (great eyebrows - eerie, too) - glue on a happy face

4. Tie ribbons around the neck and a bell if you have one.

OR

tie a nice scarf around the neck.

- These are great fun when you make bunches of them with bunches of people - make one of each person - have fun!

finger puppets III

So cute · so tidy · so clean to do! make a family of these dainties – one for each finger of your hand.

1. Cut up squares of cotton fabrics - muslin is nice, but small, light, calico-type prints will give you a raggedy-Anne effect.
2. Drop a cotton ball in the center and wrap fabric over cotton to form the head
3. Now, secure the head with a rubber band, leaving enough stretch for you to slip your finger under it. (Like the old ghosts we used to make)
4. Stitch on tiny bead eyes or sequin eyes.
5. glue on a yarn mouth and yarn or cotton hair.
6. Make felt arms and legs and glue or stitch onto skirt. Decorate skirt with beads, yarn and sequins.

CREPE PAPER PUPPETS

These merry creatures are a visual delight!

1. Wrap an 18" by 18" square of crepe paper over a tightly wadded ball of newspaper.
2. Secure at base with a 18" piece of roving which will create arms.
   ~ for a lady, simply trim off excess to form a skirt and make felt legs ~ glue to inside of dress.
   ~ for a gentleman, slit skirt halfway up and separate to form legs ~ tie with yarn in various places; tie at waist.
3. Using felt, develop facial expression, hands, hair, hats and buttons.
4. Make them holding a treasure!

SWINGERS

1. Cut a simple body out of oaktag ~ arms out!
2. Color summer clothes on; add an expression to your swinger.
3. Run a 3 foot piece of roving through a painted toilet paper tube and knot on top ~ staple arms to roving.
4. Fold figure slightly so it sits onto seat ~ add a dab of glue
5. Attach a balloon from hand to roving.

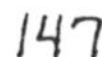

MOLDED PUPPETS

cotton stuffing

Stitch hands inside sleeve.

CREATIVE CHARACTERS are well-suited to this method of puppetry. Because the mixture to create the head may be modeled, lots of different possibilities emerge for characterizations.

poke a hole in neck — make certain you have enough around the hole for support.

Recipe for HEAD (and hands):

1 part wheat (wallpaper) paste
2 parts sawdust

} mix together, then gradually add water til mixture becomes putty.

★ mixture is not really pliable ★
- don't attempt delicate stuff - go for substantial features.
- dry on wax paper.

Construction

1. Shape head - exaggerate features and form a nice sturdy neck - push a hole up from bottom of neck so you can stick your finger in.
2. Make hands - poke little holes through top of hands for connection later.
3. Design costume appropriate to character. Stitch sides and turn inside out.
4. After head and hands dry, paint with temperas then shellac.
5. Make yarn, steel wool or cotton hair, and a head piece - hat, scarf, etc.
6. Connect hands to arms of costume through holes - stitch together; stuff arms with cotton; glue around neck area, slip in costume - tie with yarn to reinforce.

TUBE PEOPLE

Simple as can be, these tube characters can be made for any holiday and serve as name markers, hung as ornaments, set on cupboard shelves.

1. Paint a toilet paper tube or make a costume to cover it from paper or felt. - add lots of props and details - cookies and milk for Santa, a badge and a gun for the marshal, a pot of gold for the Leprechaun.
2. Cut head with substantial neck-tape to inside of tube - glue on features - make yarn hair, bead eyes, a burlap or felt hat.
3. Cut arms and legs - make colorful stockings and glue onto tube.

Ashanti Dolls

Make a puppet symbolic of these wooden dolls, characteristic of the Ashanti tribe in Ghana. The round head on these girls' dolls represents beauty. Older women carried these figures in the backs of their skirts to ensure well formed children.

1. Cut head with neck from corrugated cardboard.
2. Pad and tape with newspaper to give a little fullness to head.
3. Insert inside paper toweling tube-tape. Tape on egg carton sections for arms. Bend a piece of corrugated cardboard to fit around bottom of tube. (This helps balance the doll.) Tape.
4. Coat the entire figure with either Paris Craft strips or papier-mâché strips. *Smooth out!!*
5. When dry, paint with brown temperas. Shellac.
6. Glue on black felt features, tie rope, jute, beads and feathers around neck area. Add a strand of beads to bottom section. Use crude, natural decorative materials.

foil puppets

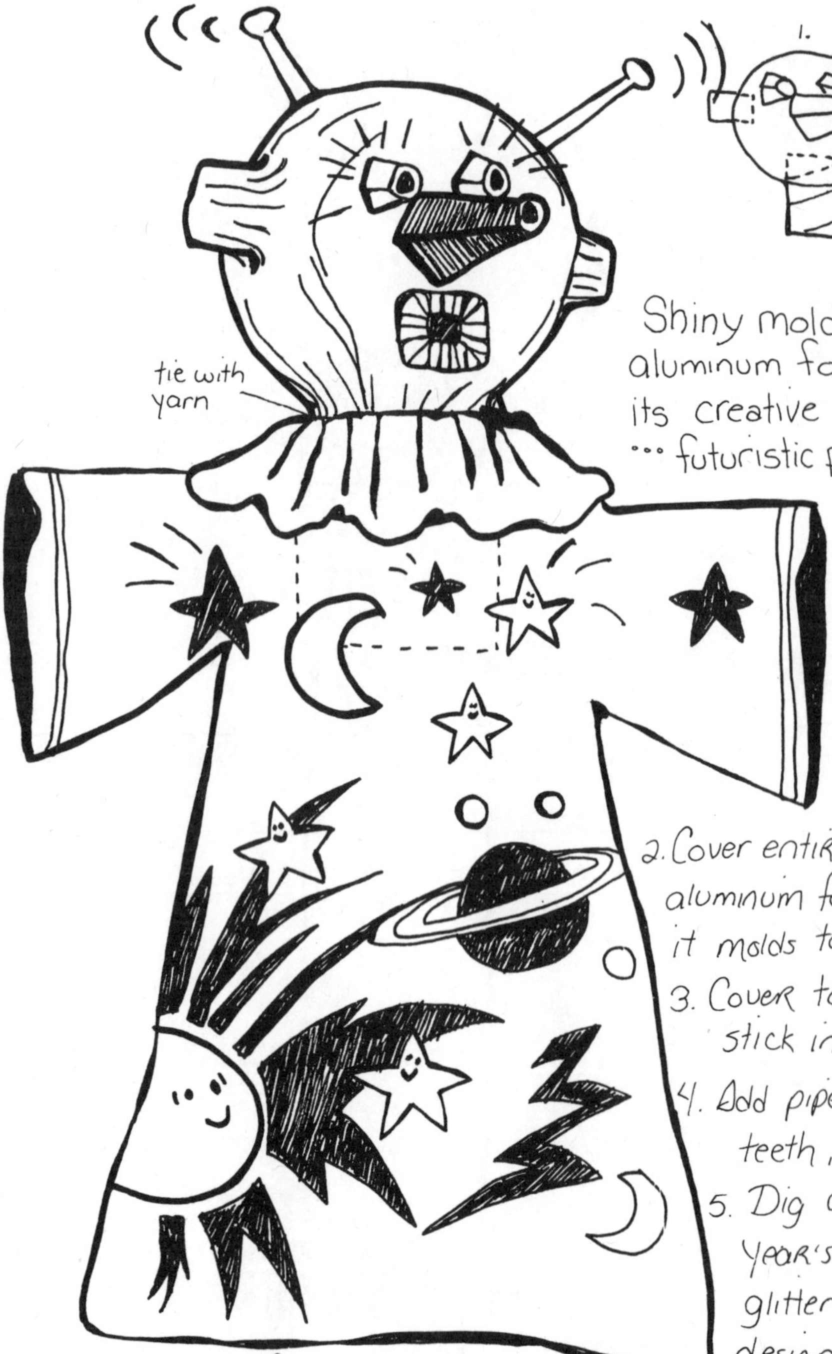

Shiny moldable aluminum foil finds its creative potential... ...futuristic puppets!

1. Create puppet's features by pressing egg carton cups, toweling tube sections or cut corrugated cardboard shapes into a 3" styrofoam ball. Push in a tube section for neck.
2. Cover entire head, including neck, with aluminum foil - press foil real well, so it molds to contour of features.
3. Cover toothpicks with foil and stick in for antennae.
4. Add pipe cleaners for hair, lashes, teeth, etc.
5. Dig up your Mom's old New Year's Eve dresses - the gold, glittery, shimmery stuff - and design a spacey costume. Sides can be hand stitched then turned inside-out.
6. Stitch on final embellishments - sequins, stars, glitter, etc.
7. Attach costume by slipping neck in, tying securely, then folding down fabric to make a collar.

PARIS CRAFT PUPPETS

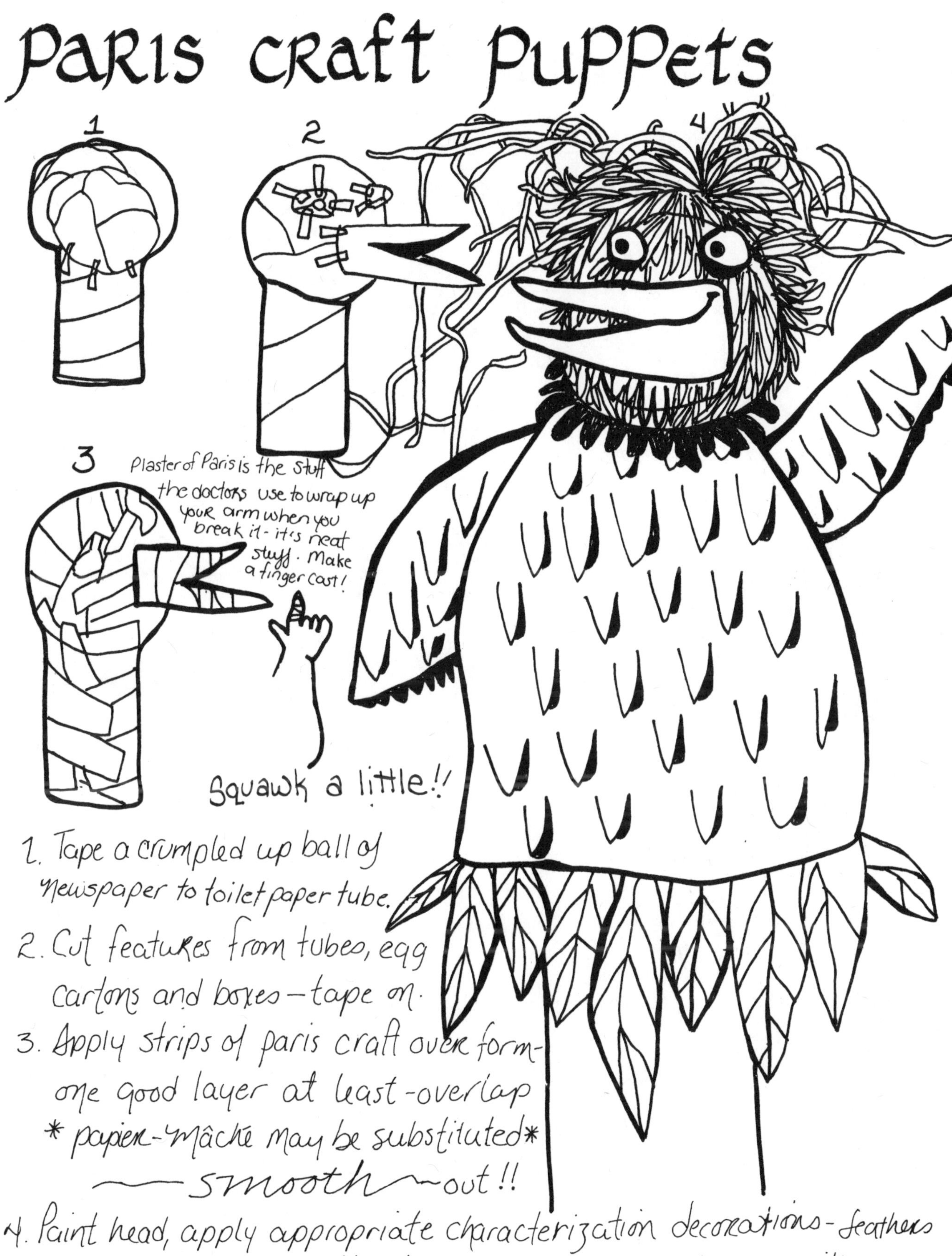

1. Tape a crumpled up ball of newspaper to toilet paper tube.
2. Cut features from tubes, egg cartons and boxes—tape on.
3. Apply strips of paris craft over form—one good layer at least—overlap
   * papier-mâché may be substituted *
   —— smooth —— out!!
4. Paint head, apply appropriate characterization decorations—feathers fur; attach a cloth skirt to neck with glue and secure with yarn.

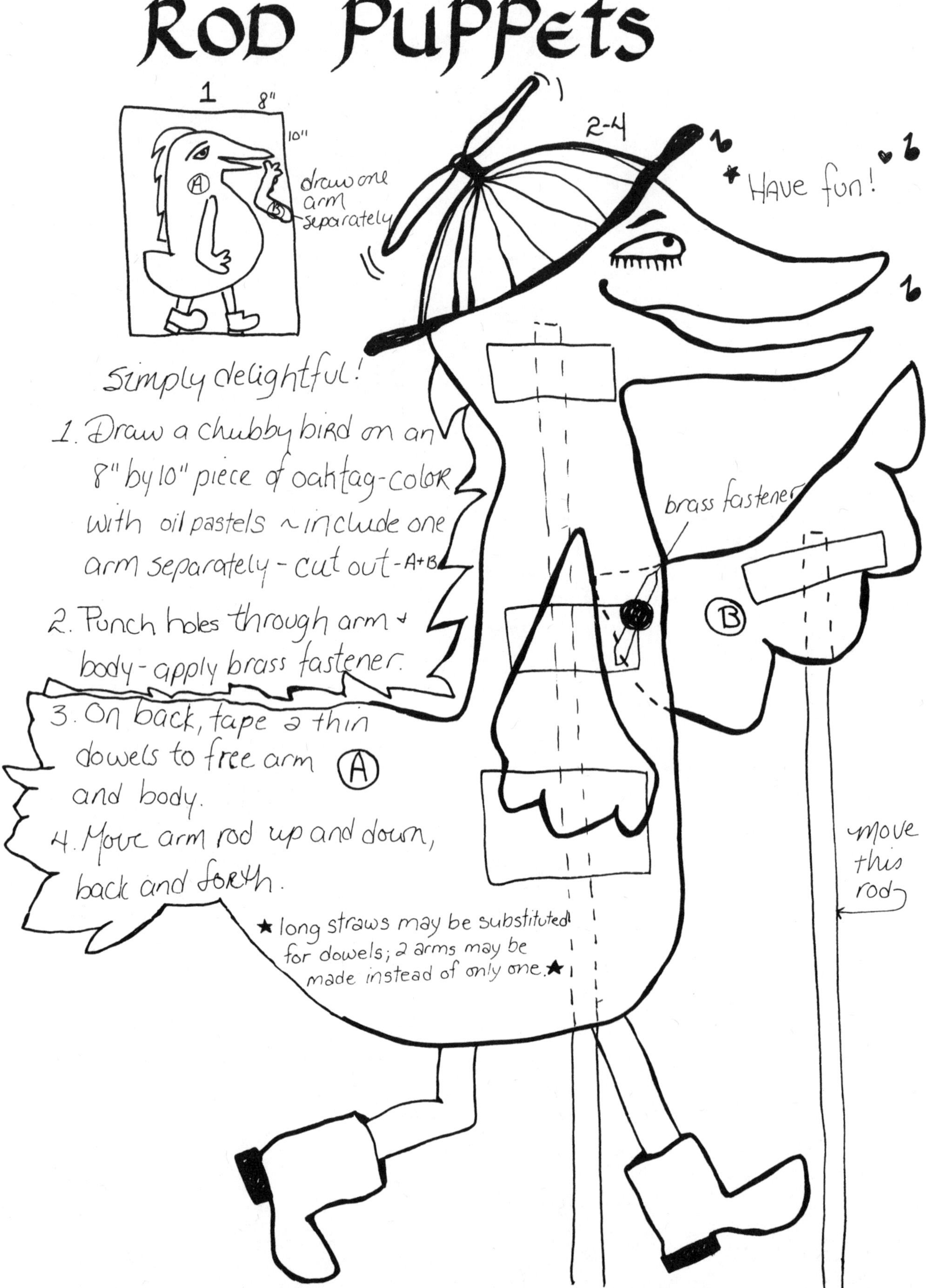
ROD PUPPETS
1
8"
10"
draw one arm separately
A
B
2-4
Have fun!
Simply delightful!
1. Draw a chubby bird on an 8" by 10" piece of oaktag-color with oil pastels ~ include one arm separately - cut out - A+B
2. Punch holes through arm + body - apply brass fastener.
3. On back, tape 2 thin dowels to free arm and body.
4. Move arm rod up and down, back and forth.
brass fastener
★ long straws may be substituted for dowels; 2 arms may be made instead of only one. ★
move this rod

Spread your wings and let the sun shine in ★ don't hesitate ~~→ create!

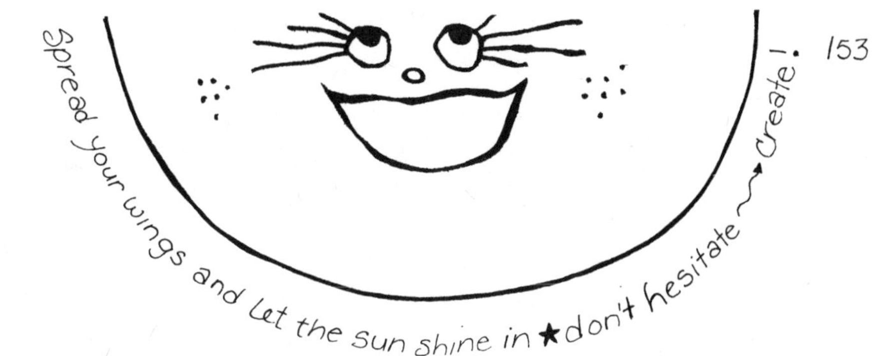

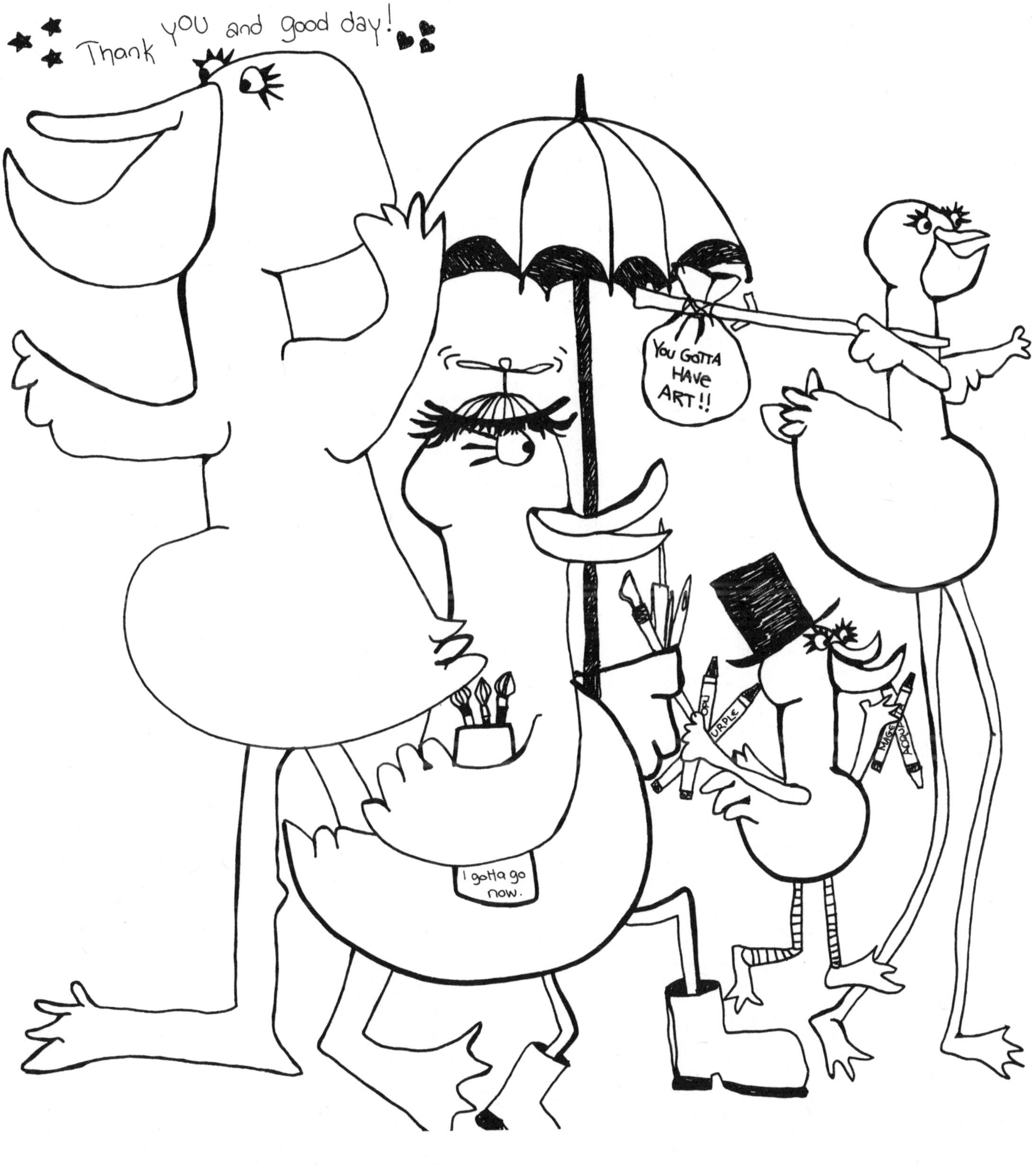
Thank YOU and good day!
YOU GOTTA HAVE ART!!
I gotta go now.

WE'VE only just begun! get those wheels moving and one creation leads to another! How do you think I wrote this book?

SoME CREATIVE KinDLERS:

1. turn old favorite clothes into fun by:
   - ♥ making fun patches out of outgrown jeans for favorite jeans, flannel shirts or coveralls.
   - ♥ design and embroider a fantasy trip on a soft plain shirt.
   - ♥ do a fabric crayon masterpiece on a white t-shirt to symbolize your secret society!
   - ♥ re-cycle a discolored, faded, or stained shirt or skirt with a dye bath- or, tie-dye it!
2. Recycle those wonderful chenille bedspreads! make skirts, jackets, tops and totebags. from simple patterns. Do the same with old drapes and tableclothes.
3. Use that nice, thick upholstery fabric from discarded sofas for simple carry-all bags - make nice long shoulder straps and a couple of compartments on the outside.
4. Spray paint old wicker baskets - from fruit or Bermuda - and hook them for clothes pins or mail.
5. Cover cigar boxes with wallpaper - use them to contain buttons, nc-rac and art treasures.
6. Make a natural mobile from the lovelies collected on a beach walk - make a driftwood support and suspend shells, wood and rocks.

7. Make sachets from your summer roses and old lace and ribbons.
8. Turn those cracked cups and mugs into cactus pots.
9. Cover worn spots on chair and sofa backs with lovely flea market doilies. Do the same for pillows.
10. Store partially opened pasta, grains and cereals in old jars-they're beautiful and functional!
11. Stitch a puppet face on each finger of that odd woolen glove.
12. Cover coffee cans with felt-make an animated face on it and use it on your gas stove or wood stove to hold matches.
13. Paint a beautiful, smooth rock and use it as a door stop or paper weight. Make an animal from it.
14. Use old toys to make new ones-collect parts from a variety of trucks or dolls and put them together to create a totally inventive model.
15. Frame a calendar print-ecology calendars are beautiful!
16. Fill plastic eggs with nuts and raisins-tie a yellow and purple ribbon around the middle and give them to friends.
17. Make a bird house by cutting a couple of holes in dried out gourds-hang them from a tree.
18. Feed your fine feathered friends by securing some wire to a tightly knit-type pine cone and then coating the cone with peanut butter-hang it outside.
19. Make a huge totem pole with odd size tin cans taped together and embellished with egg carton features Mâché and paint!

20. Spray paint old pie tins black. Stencil a bright enamel design on them use hex signs for ideas. Hang on your wall.
21. Spend the afternoon collecting wild flowers. Press them in heavy books. Mount and insert under glass in wooden frame.... or, sandwich between two pieces of glass.
22. Make cozy pillow cases from leftover flannel.
23. Have an art swap - call your friends together and barter art supplies - exchange ideas too.
24. Make a family tree collage from the old photographs hanging around - add traces of memorabilia, like netting from nonny's hat, flowers from Lena's corsage or lace from an antique undergarment. Mount on Masonite and frame under glass.
25. Using acrylics, paint delicate flowers to brighten up all those old wooden kitchen spoons and forks.

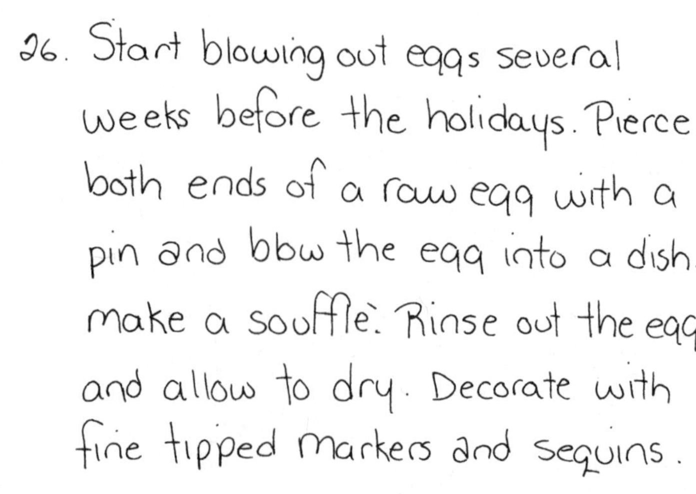

26. Start blowing out eggs several weeks before the holidays. Pierce both ends of a raw egg with a pin and blow the egg into a dish - make a soufflé. Rinse out the egg and allow to dry. Decorate with fine tipped markers and sequins.

27. Replace your old sneaker laces with a rainbow pair.

Helpful Hints

1. Different glues serve different purposes.
   - Rubber cement is especially good when gluing thin paper to a surface - it won't warp the paper.
   - White glue is great for nearly everything else. It joins wood, plastic, cardboard, pottery and fixes objects made of these materials.

2. Substitute white glue for stitching when making small stuffed forms - it simplifies lessons so that they may be directed toward younger children.

3. Nice straight branches may be substituted for many projects requiring dowels.

4. Old broom and mop handles make great dowels when a sturdy one is called for.

5. Soft art requires mounds of stuffing and can become expensive. Be creative in locating sources of substitute stuffing. Use stuffing from old pillows, stuffed toys and batting from couches and stuffed arm chairs.

6. Frequent flea markets and tag sales for cheap supplies.

7. Tear apart those New Years' Eve gowns collecting dust in those garment bags. You'll retrieve sequins, braiding, beads, cording and shimmery, exciting fabric to use on futuristic puppets or Halloween costumes or hanging fish.

8. Save those tresses from your next haircut and make a look-alike puppet.

9. Locate the scrap suppliers in the area - furniture stores are sources of great upholstery samples, paint and wallpaper outlets will gladly donate last year's sample books, and many lumber yards are happy to unload bits of scrap wood.

10. Break apart beaded belts, bags and jewelry for a wealth of assorted beads.

11. Fake fur trim from discarded coats makes wonderful animal fur.

12. Empty detergent bottles make great paint dispensers.

13. Egg cartons hold twelve different colors. They may also be used to teach color mixing.

14. Add a few drops of liquid detergent to tempera paint if you want to paint tin foil.

15. Vitamin bottles are perfect storage containers for decorative trim such as glitter, sequins, beads and wiggly eyes.

16. Use styrofoam egg cartons and meat trays for experimental and creative stitchery. Various levels allow for interesting effects.

17. Utilize large appliance boxes for stage settings, puppet stages and model homes.

18. Recruit those out of date bean bag chairs. They'll serve as an endless supply for bean bag toss animals or weigh down soft art sculptures.

19. For interesting effects with common subject matter, dwarf or blow up an object! Papier-mâché a giant carpenter ant dwarfing a 6 inch elephant. Use opaque projectors to enlarge ordinary things to achieve extra-ordinary effects – vegetables, insects and birds.

20. Discarded, polyfiberfill bedspreads may be substituted where synthetic batting is called for.

RECIPES

Edible Pretzels - these can be rolled into ornaments, ducks, birds, numbers and letters and the best part is in the eatin' - YUM!

(honey may be added). 1 C. warm water, 1 package of yeast } mix and sit for a few minutes.

Next, add 1 T. salt and 2½ C. whole wheat pastry flour. Mix and knead, then roll dough into shapes. Place on lightly greased cookie sheet and bake in a preheated oven at 425° for 12 minutes or until browned.

- if you want a shiny glazed pretzel, beat an egg and brush on shapes before baking.

Clay Dough - food coloring can be mixed in for color.

1 C. flour, 1 T. alum, 1 C. water } mix to the consistency of putty adding more water or flour.

Salt Ceramic Dough

mix 1 C. salt and ½ C. cornstarch and add ¾ C. cold water. - cook mixture in double boiler until a bread dough consistency is achieved - about two minutes. Cool on wax paper and knead for several minutes. Dough will keep for several days when wrapped in plastic bags.

Papier-Mâché Pulp - good for landscapes - paint when dry.

1 shredded newspaper - really shred it.
6 T. flour
1 C. liquid starch

knead mixture until heavy dough consistency is achieved - the longer the mixture sits the thicker it will become and the more the newspaper will break down.

Salt Clay - good for making little beads. Food coloring may be added when mixed.

1 C. salt
½ C. flour
} add water until dough like consistency results.

Plaster Carving Blocks

mix 2 parts plaster of Paris to 1 part sawdust. Sprinkle mixture into a bowl which has a little water in it. When mixture rises above water level, stir with fingers and pour into waxed milk cartons. when dry, tear off carton and carve with table knife. Use sandpaper to smooth.

Sandpaper - good as a background for sandpainting

Brush a mixture of white glue diluted with water on corrugated cardboard. Sprinkle on beach sand - shake off extra.

Colored Sand - good for sand painting or layered in jars. mix powdered tempera paint with salt or fine beach sand. Intensity is achieved by the degree of paint mixed in.

Mock Oil Paint - mix wheat paste to a thin consistency. Add powdered tempera paint and paint with a stiff brush.

Marbled Paper - mix a little powdered tempera paint into a small quantity of turpentine. Pour mixture into a sink filled with water and gently swirl water to achieve an exciting pattern. Place a sheet of white paper on top of mixture. Peel paper off and your pattern will have transferred itself to paper. Use to wrap small presents.

Papier-Mâché Paste - if you're in a pinch and have no wallpaper paste, flour may be mixed with water to give you a poor substitute for mâché paste.

Paris Craft - thin gauze or cheezecloth may be cut into strips and dipped into a thin plaster of Paris mixture. If utilized quickly, this method works well in covering a sculptural armature. A nice drapery quality can be achieved.

Inspirational Art Books

Debelak, Marianne; Herr, Judith; and Jacobson, Martha. Creating Innovative Classroom Materials For Teaching Young Children. Harcourt Brace Jovanovich Inc., New York, 1981.

Eager, Fred. The Italic Way to Beautiful Handwriting. Macmillan Publishing Co; Inc., New York, 1974.

Fiarotta, Phyllis and Fiarotta, Noel. Confetti. Workman Publishing Co., New York, 1978.

Kennedy, Paul C. North American Indian Design Coloring Book. Dover Publications, Inc., New York, 1971.

Laury, Jean Ray and Aiken, Joyce. The Pantyhose Craft Book. Paplinger Publishing. Co., New York, 1978.

Linderman, Earl W. Teaching Secondary School Art. Wm. C. Brown Company Publishers, Dubuque, Iowa, 1971.

Lothrop, Samuel Kirkland. Pre-Columbian Designs from Panama. Dover Publications, Inc., New York, 1976.

Lowenfeld, Viktor and Brittain, Lambert W. Creative and Mental growth. Macmillan Company, New York, 1967.

Parrinder, Geoffrey. African Mythology. Hamlyn Publishing Group Ltd., London, 1967.

Romberg, Jenean and Rutz, Miriam Easton. Art Today and EveryDay: Classroom Activities For the Elementary School Year. Parker Publishing Company, Inc., New York, 1972.

Scharf, Sol. Holiday Treasure Chest. KTAV Publishing House, New York, 1978.

Scott, Toni. The Complete Book of Stuffed Work. Houghton Mifflin
Co

St ...ir Extraordinary History.
(

Str ... Anti-Coloring Book.
F ... , 1978.

Wa ... rper and Row Publishers,

Wa ... igg, Marietta. A Handbook
... pany Publishers, Dubuque,

W ... ditional Sourses. Dover

W ... sn and Co., Boston, 1973